"It is a privilege to meet Diane Cameron through this book. She has made her own hero's journey and brought us back this boon. No sentimentality here!"

Jonathan Shay, MD, PhD
Author of *Achilles in Vietnam* and *Odysseus in America*

★ ★ ★

"Wars never end for their survivors. Military trauma all too often devastates the lives of our veterans and those who love them long after armistice. With this poignant, timely, and unforgettable memoir of her own effort to comprehend, Diane Cameron issues a powerful reminder that mental trauma is an intricate, three-dimensional problem—one that resists easy judgments and defies simple answers. Grounded in history, informed by psychiatry, and written with a rare blend of compassion and moral urgency, this is a powerful meditation on love, war, and our humanity. As our young men and women continue to return from Iraq and Afghanistan, may their families—and our national policy makers—read this important book and ponder its many valuable insights."

Brian Matthew Jordan, PhD
Author of *Marching Home: Union Veterans and
Their Unending Civil War*

"Diane Cameron's *Never Leave Your Dead*, unfolding like a good psychological mystery, is at once heartfelt and unillusioned. It asks the hard questions and considers the harrowing evidence about violence and its impacts on the soul but then looks to move past judgment. To understand the power of forgiveness we need to understand what things need to be forgiven. Cameron instructs us in both."

Sven Birkerts
Author of *The Gutenberg Elegies* and *The Art of the Memoir*

★ ★ ★

"If you have ever wondered about and tried to understand what motivates victims of psychological trauma to commit acts of violence, this book is for you. Cameron takes you with her on her journey of discovery, finding records and talking to experts to put the pieces of the puzzle of her stepfather together. *Never Leave Your Dead* helps the reader to understand that sometimes perpetrators of violence are victims of, and witnesses to, the most horrendous indecency human beings can inflict on one another. I highly recommend this work as an effort toward a greater understanding of individuals suffering from PTSD who might commit acts of violence."

Victor Ashear, PhD
Author of *Self-Acceptance: The Key to Recovery from Mental Illness*

★ ★ ★

"Part memoir, part history lesson, and part psychological mystery, Diane Cameron's book educates all of us about the complexity of a single life, and she helps us to understand and honor our warriors, past and present. As a clinician who worked with traumatized veterans at the VA for many years, I am moved by the compassion in Diane's understanding of what it means to be a Marine and how the trauma of war can mold one's life forever."

Susan Griffiths, RN, MS
Clinical Nurse Specialist in Psychiatric Nursing

★ ★ ★

"Diane Cameron's book is a tour de force—with the page-turning power of a world-class thriller. It is the story of one family member's attempt to create a coherent narrative out of the mind-numbing shards of war trauma. Cameron is a fierce detective—deeply well-informed—and every page of her determined inquiry moves us closer to a nuanced understanding of the effects of trauma on us all. I simply could not put this book down."

Stephen Cope
Senior Scholar-in-Residence at Kripalu Center for Yoga and Health and best-selling author of *The Great Work of Your Life* and *Yoga and the Quest for the True Self*

NEVER
LEAVE
YOUR
DEAD

NEVER LEAVE YOUR DEAD

A True Story of War Trauma, Murder, and Madness

Diane Cameron

CENTRAL RECOVERY PRESS

LAS VEGAS

Central Recovery Press (CRP) is committed to publishing exceptional materials addressing addiction treatment, recovery, and behavioral healthcare topics.

For more information, visit www.centralrecoverypress.com.

Publisher: Central Recovery Press
              3321 N. Buffalo Drive
              Las Vegas, NV 89129

21 20 19 18 17 16   1 2 3 4 5

Library of Congress Cataloging-in-Publication Data

Name: Cameron, Diane.
Title: Never leave your dead: a true story of war trauma, murder, and madness / Diane Cameron.
Description: Las Vegas, NV: Central Recovery Press, 2016. | Description based on print version record and CIP data provided by publisher; resource not viewed.
Identifiers: LCCN 2015050654 (print) | LCCN 2015048731 (ebook) | ISBN 9781942094173 (ebook) | ISBN 9781942094166 (paperback)
Subjects: LCSH: Watkins, Donald K., 1911–1996. | Cameron, Diane—Family. | Marines—United States—Biography. | Sino-Japanese War, 1937–1945— Psychological aspects. | Stepfathers—United States—Biography. | Mothers and daughters—United States—Biography. | Veterans—Mental health—United States—Case studies. | Post-traumatic stress disorder—United States—Case studies. | Mentally ill—Family relationships—United States—Case studies. | Murder—Pennsylvania—Washington County—History—20th century. | BISAC: BIOGRAPHY & AUTOBIOGRAPHY / Personal Memoirs. | PSYCHOLOGY / Psychopathology / Post-Traumatic Stress Disorder (PTSD). | TRUE CRIME / Murder / General.
Classification: LCC VE25.W38 (print) | LCC VE25.W38 C36 2016 (ebook) | DDC 616.85/210092—dc23
LC record available at http://lccn.loc.gov/2015050654

Photo of Diane Cameron by Cindy Schultz

Horrors of War card used courtesy of The Topps Company, Inc. For more information about The Topps Company, please see our website at www.topps.com.

Washington Observer excerpts and headlines used courtesy of the *Observer Reporter*.

Reprinted with the permission of Simon & Schuster, Inc. from COLD STORAGE by Wendell Rawls, Jr. Copyright ©1980 by Wendell Rawls, Jr. All rights reserved.

Cover and interior design and layout by Sara Streifel, Think Creative Design

In honor of the
United States China Marines

&

in memory of
Lawrence Edward Oklota

Ships that pass in the night, and speak each other in passing,

Only a signal shown and a distant voice in the darkness;

So on the ocean of life we pass and speak one another,

Only a look and a voice, then darkness again and a silence.

—**Henry Wadsworth Longfellow,** "The Theologian's Tale: Elizabeth"

TABLE OF CONTENTS

Diane Cameron has enlarged my understanding of what it means to be a warrior. The stories she recounts of United States Marines stationed in China during the Japanese invasion and occupation at the beginning of World War II certainly illustrate one of the fundamental roles played by the profession of arms in our society—to protect life, property, commerce, and our national identity. Also the stories in this book suggest ways in which war can inflict deep and lasting psychological wounds in warriors. Yet the greatest lesson in *Never Leave Your Dead* is how the way of the warrior emerges not from the lives of the author's beloved China Marines but from her own pilgrimage to imagine and understand the tragic life of one particular China Marine—the one who married her mother years later— and to bring home his memory, finally, with love and honor.

Whether engaged in warfare, peacekeeping, or humanitarian assistance, the greatest challenges warriors face are moral rather than physical. For deployed warriors, physical dangers come and go, but moral dangers are everywhere, all the time. In the high-stakes world of the warrior, there is usually one, or perhaps just a few, right things to do in each situation. And both the cost and consequences of those right actions can be enormous. For a Marine on guard duty, the right thing is to find every threat to those being guarded and to let none pass. For a Navy corpsman tending the wounds of Marines on a battlefield, the right thing is to save every life and limb. For a China Marine in Shanghai in 1937, the right thing was to do nothing—to merely watch as thousands were raped and killed. That's not a tough job; it's an impossible job. We now know that one of the consequences of failing to live up to one's own moral expectation can be moral injury, a deep and lasting wound to one's personal identity.

At a deeper level, perhaps the warrior's challenge is more than just choosing right actions over wrong. Perhaps the most fundamental role warriors play in our society is to venture into the unclaimed territory between good and evil, to construct goodness right there on evil's doorstep, and then to defend it with their lives. To serve selflessly while others exploit, to show compassion while others are cruel, to forgive the unforgiveable—these are all ways to create goodness in the face of evil. So also is making sense of a brutal double murder that happened decades ago in order to find and celebrate the humanity of a veteran China Marine.

This book is a creation of goodness on the doorstep of evil. And its author is as much a warrior as the Marines she writes about, even though she has never worn a uniform.

—William P. Nash, MD
Director of Psychological Health
United States Marine Corps

This is the story of Donald Watkins, the man my mother married when she was seventy years old. He was a Marine, a murderer, and a former mental patient. At first I wondered, *How could she marry this man?* Today I understand why, because long after his death, I love Donald too.

But it wasn't love at first sight. Two years after Donald's death I was given a box of his papers, and my search for the truth of this tragic man began. I journeyed long and far. I met amazing people in unusual places. I had to learn their stories so I could finally understand Donald.

Donald was not the only one with problems. Our family had many challenges, and over the generations we took trauma and compounded it. But to my great surprise, as I undertook this pilgrimage to understand him, I was changed.

We were not a military family, so I had to confront the misconceptions and stereotypes I had about those who make a commitment to military life. I had to search archives and libraries and I had to find experts to translate the facts of Donald's life, encountering revelations every step along the way.

I found documents, reports, records, and ephemera: menus, baseball programs, bits of old film, and parts of American history I never learned in school. Also, I found teachers. My most important teachers were a group of courageous men who were old, sometimes deaf or blind, but who had an abundance of fortitude, resilience, humor, and honor. These were United States China Marines.

I learned two important lessons from my teachers—both the experts on trauma and the men who lived it: First, trauma is not the terrible thing that happens to you, but what is left inside you because it happened. And second, if something terrible happens to you, that is not the story. How you survive and how you love and are loved again is the story.

As you read this book you will see that the story is told out of order, because I learned Donald's story out of order, but also because trauma—whether from war or crime or abuse—always and tragically leaves us out of order. You will also see I have included scenes that, to the best of my understanding, represent insights into what Donald experienced. I built these scenes from conversations with Donald, with my mother, with other China Marines, with survivors of mental institutions, and with those who directly participated in Donald's liberation.

The Murder—March 7, 1953

He came into the basement through the cellar door and headed directly to the gun case over his woodworking bench. He was still wearing his gray jacket and the blue tie with maroon swirls that his wife had given him last year for his new job as the English teacher at Washington Valley High School.

He removed the gun from the case and weighed it for a moment with both hands before he began to load it. He hadn't fired a gun since hunting last fall and, before that, since he was a Marine in China.

He closed the case quietly and walked up the stairs. He could hear his mother-in-law in the kitchen; she was starting dinner. She removed dishes from the cupboard, the oven door banged, and a utensil clattered to the floor.

He had left school early that day and gone to walk in the woods again. Recently, he'd been doing this more and more. Sometimes he told the principal he was sick. But lately, he'd leave the classroom and walk straight out of the school. Something would come over him when he looked at the boys and girls in his class, and he'd get a sour taste in his mouth. And then the foggy feeling would come.

When he walked in the woods, it helped. He'd think about China or try not to think about it. But when that foggy feeling came, the pictures would just slip into his vision. He'd see the bodies, and sometimes only severed arms and legs. The worst were the babies, limp and dead. Some were cut in half. It took so much energy to push these pictures out of his head. They seemed always to be on the edge of his vision. If he closed his eyes, they just stayed. He was exhausted from trying not to see the images that tortured him.

In the past week or so, a new thought had come to him with the pictures. It was confusing. He had this idea—it was like a fact, very certain—that his wife was in danger, right here in Pennsylvania, not China. What made it more confusing was that he knew his mother-in-law was the danger. That was very clear.

His mother-in-law would always yell at him when he came home early from school.

"You'll get fired," she'd scream at him.

And she told his wife that he was crazy.

"You know he thinks you're unfaithful. Only a crazy person would believe that," she'd say, raising her voice.

When she yelled, he got mad, and that made the pictures in his head more confusing: China, the kids in his class, his wife, the dead bodies, and his mother-in-law yelling. They all rolled together.

He could no longer think about all these pressures. He had the gun in his hands; he was at the top of the stairs now. It was past three o'clock in the afternoon. His wife would be home in half an hour. Best to do this fast, make this pain stop. He stepped into the kitchen; his mother-in-law looked up. She was wearing a yellow apron, holding a mixing bowl. She looked surprised. The stove was on; the oven was warming up. She started to look at the clock as he raised the gun and aimed directly at her face. Blood splattered everywhere.

The sound of the gun surprised him, but when he looked at her lying on the floor—her apron not so yellow anymore—he felt an odd comfort. This scene was familiar. He saw his mother-in-law, but he also saw the women's bodies on the streets in Shanghai, layered images moving in and out of here and there.

He always saw more women's bodies than men's. The Japanese stacked the men in groups so their bodies were tangled in enormous piles, but the women's bodies could be seen in doorways, fields, and alleys—everywhere. The worst was finding arms or legs but no body. Sometimes there would be a woman on the side of the road who had been dissected or had a stick or bottle shoved inside one of her orifices.

He glanced at the clock. His wife would be home soon. He loved her so much. All he wanted was to be with her, be happy, and feel better. He knew that today was trouble. He understood what he had just done, but what else could he do? He knew he'd have to go to jail. That was another problem: He loved his wife; he couldn't be separated from her. And she needed him; she depended on him. A wave of fear and sadness went through him. She was young and pretty. Other men would want her. She might even want another man. Anger flowed on top of the fear. He bent over and picked up the dish towel that had fallen near his mother-in-law's body. Then he wiped the gun.

He took the extra cartridges from his pocket and finished reloading just as he heard his wife come through the front door. She always came in that way, after stopping to get the mail from out front. She was now in the living room. He met her halfway; he didn't want her to see her mother on the floor and be frightened. He dropped his head and started to cry.

There was no alternative; he knew that. She looked at him, and her mouth started to open, no words. He could barely meet her eyes as he raised the gun. He fired at her chest, and she crossed her arms, almost a gesture of modesty, as she fell backward. He shot again, aiming down at her heart. He was crying openly now as he fired more shots at her chest and neck. He could never shoot her head; she was so pretty.

When her body was still, he knelt and straightened her bloodstained dress. He gently laid the gun away from her body. Then he rose and walked calmly to the kitchen, avoiding the sight of his faceless mother-in-law. He continued on his path and turned off the stove.

He pulled a kitchen chair over to the corner of the room and removed the telephone receiver from its cradle on the wall. He calmly asked the operator to connect him to the Washington County Sheriff. He needed to sit down. Suddenly he was so tired.

CHAPTER ONE

My Mother's Donald

I sensed Donald's entry into my mother's life before I actually met him. It was the spring of 1984, and I was living in Washington, DC. I had the habit of waking on Sundays to my mother's regular phone call from Pittsburgh. But one Sunday I noticed, well into the evening, that my mother hadn't called. I left a message on her answering machine to check in, and when I called her later that week she said she couldn't talk long; she was going out. That was new. Something had changed.

When I mentioned that she seemed to be busier than usual, she said, "Yes, well, I have plans," and laughed.

I called my brother Larry, who also lived in Pittsburgh, to see if he had any more information. "Mum has plans?" I asked.

"Yeah," he said, "she met this man, a really old guy. He has a farm out in Washington County. She says he was a Marine."

I was happy for my mother and happy for me. If my mother had a boyfriend, it might mean she'd leave me alone. I was recently divorced and making a new life and wanted some distance from my mother's neediness. My mother had been widowed for thirteen years. My father—her husband of thirty years—had died in 1971. He was fifty-six years old when he passed away, and I was seventeen—the last of their five children still at home. I saw my mother's grief up close and watched as she made the transition from married mother of five to single older woman. It wasn't easy for her, and I hated being the sponge for all her grief.

Part of my mother's pain was that she hated to be alone. An extravert, with no use for introspection, she needed the company of people. Growing up, I heard my mother talk about her lonely childhood. Her parents, Frank and Josephine, both worked long hours—her father was a machinist, and her mother rolled cigars in a factory. When her father was out of work during the Great Depression, her mother played poker every night—quite successfully. She went out to smoky card halls and brought home money to keep food on their table.

Consequently, my mother coped by promising herself that when she grew up, she would have a big family and give herself the brothers and sisters she longed for. We, two boys and three girls, were her promised "siblings." So when she was widowed at the age of fifty-six, as all her children were leaving home, her loneliness was doubled.

Perhaps it does not need to be said that a woman who had five children to replace her fantasized siblings might have gotten off on the wrong foot as a parent. But that is the least of it. In her pain—from her childhood, certainly, and from other causes—my mother grabbed at many salves for her misery.

My father's family had been poor, and he went to work at fourteen years old to support his six brothers and sisters. In their marriage, my father's childhood poverty and large family ran headlong into my mother's childhood loneliness.

My mother, fighting her childhood ghosts, was determined to have her large family. My father, recalling the crowded rooms his family had shared and the pain of real hunger, dreamed only of financial security. He worked constantly, rising in his career as an industrial engineer. My parents' pasts were dueling with each other. As my mother got more insistent on a big family, my father withdrew into his work and worry about money.

I was born when my mother was thirty-eight years old, and her frustration peaked soon after as it became clear that making more babies was time limited, and these five faux siblings could not soothe her loneliness.

On a visit to our family doctor when she was fifty years old, she complained that she was feeling sad and tired. Dr. Heck, who had treated all of us for chicken pox and measles, wrote my mother a prescription to boost her energy. She began taking the amphetamine Dexedrine when I was ten years old. Before my eleventh birthday, she was a full-blown drug addict.

My father was traveling during those years. He was an engineer in the corrugated box industry. He left home at 6:00 p.m. on Sunday nights to drive to Ohio, New Jersey, or New York, and he'd return on Friday night in time for supper and to attend choir practice at our United Methodist Church.

Life with a speed-addicted mother was unpredictable, to say the least. The Dexedrine ran our household. My mother was full of false energy all day, and then she crashed horribly at night.

Each morning she'd wake groggy and disoriented, and it would take her an hour to get her bearings. I learned to be careful in those morning hours, waiting to see what my mother could remember of the night before. It could go one of two ways. She might, on seeing the damage she had done—clothing and dishes strewn about the house—be remorseful and ashamed. If this was the case it was sad to watch her, but that was the safer scenario for my brother Larry and me—we were the only two left at home. We would let her cry and then leave for school.

The other possibility was that she might become upset again, and her anger of the night before would be rekindled.

I would wait and watch and try to feel out the situation. I was prepared to shift gears quickly. I learned to assess my mother's mental state by watching her face, and I'd predict, sometimes before she was conscious of it, which way her emotional tide was moving. It could be the slightest change in her eyes or a small movement of her jaw.

I also learned, through repeated practice, how to assume a totally passive stance even when I was *very* frightened. On one occasion, when I was twelve years old, I tried to put blonde streaks in my hair using a bottle of peroxide; it was a disaster. I remember trying to wash it away, not really understanding how bleach works. But when my mother saw the orangey stripes in my hair, she began screaming, dragged me to the dining room, and shoved me in front of the large mirror over the buffet. She grabbed a sharp knife and began to saw at my hair. I was crying but I kept my eyes open, not daring to even blink as the knife flashed around my face.

Years later, while taking an Outward Bound course, I learned this is exactly what you should do if you come across a bear in the woods. The instructor said if you encounter an angry bear, you must do the opposite of what your body wants to do. He explained that if a mother bear spots a human, she will scan the person for any sign of agitation. He added that you should bring your arms to your sides, move slowly to the ground, and remain passive and immobile. "Hopefully," he said, "the bear will read that submissive posture and walk on."

As a child, that's what I did with my mother. If I could stay small—moving carefully and quietly, and never making eye contact—she often would move through her anger and then become distracted by something else, which allowed me to— very slowly—gather my things and get away.

Part of my mother's morning routine was "taking her pills." This meant some vitamins, her Dexedrine, and black coffee. On most weekday mornings, we'd head to school. But sometimes, after we'd leave, my mother's acute loneliness would kick in and in her distorted emotional scenario there were two possible villains: the lazy children who had left the house or the husband who had "abandoned" her by going to work.

If her anger swelled before the drugs kicked in, she would use the phone to punish those who had left her. There were many days when she called my school and had me sent back home. On other days my father got the calls at his office.

By nine o'clock in the morning, with the Dexedrine hitting her bloodstream, my mother transformed. I came to know this changeover quite well, witnessing it on weekends and on days when she kept me home from school. It was like superimposing another being on my mother's body.

With Dexedrine in her system, my mother became manic. She would do her hair and makeup, clean the kitchen, begin some craft projects, maybe start reading a book, and then decide to redecorate a room. She could read three newspapers, hang out several loads of laundry, and watch her soap operas while ironing baskets of clothes.

When I spent a day at home with her, my mother was full of ideas and projects. We played with makeup, sorted clothes, and sewed for my dolls. Sometimes we'd take the bus into downtown Pittsburgh to shop or see a movie—sometimes two—and have a ladies' lunch at Kaufmann's Department Store. I loved those days. She was fascinating, interesting, and fun.

But by nine o'clock at night, the Dexedrine would begin to wear off. On a good night, Larry and I would be in bed, but we'd hear my mother wandering through the house, winding down from her high-energy expenditures. She would watch television and talk to herself, and sometimes she'd cry. On bad nights, she would work herself into a rage.

When my mother began to rant about "he" and "him," I knew Larry and I were probably safe for the night, and her anger was focused on my father. She felt abandoned when he was out of town. But if she was mumbling about those "ungrateful bastards," then I knew Larry and I would need to right some perceived wrong. Often I would be dragged out of bed to clean the floor, sew on coat buttons that had been left dangling, or write a forgotten thank-you note.

There were also nights when my mother lost her grasp on reality. She might, on those nights, work herself into a fury and threaten to cut off my chubby brother's "pig flesh" or bring scissors to cut up the clothes she determined I was not sufficiently grateful for.

There were some nights when she woke us to come sit with her. Those nights were less scary but more tiring. On those nights, my mother was lonely rather than angry, and she'd talk about her childhood. She'd cry about the cold house she came home to as a girl, and her grief at her own mother's death when she was a young teenager. I didn't understand "abandonment" or "delayed grief" then, but on those nights I did understand that I could hate a person and love her at the same time.

In those years my mother and I had a relationship that fit between 9:00 a.m. and 9:00 p.m. As a kid, I thought you could set a clock by it. But as an adult, I realized you could ruin a life by it. There was little conversation in our family about my mother's addiction. We worked around her and suffered with it.

I made it to age eighteen and then moved out of the house. That same year my father died suddenly from a stroke, and six months later I married a man whom I barely knew. Looking back, I see the marriage as a straightforward escape. That husband was a man I had met at the Pittsburgh Explorers Club—a large group that made weekend trips to West Virginia and New York to hike, rock climb, and kayak. I dated him for two months, then we became engaged and married two months later. The marriage was over in less than a year.

Twenty years later, as I was sitting in a therapist's office, I made the connection between that brief marriage and the death of my father. It took me that long to see what I had done. I now have deep respect for the power of denial.

My mother continued to take Dexedrine for two more years, and then one day, by accident or an act of grace, she went to a new doctor, and when he asked her about her medications she told him the truth. He took away her Dexedrine and started her on estrogen. In less than a month, she transformed: she gained weight, her moods and body softened, and she began to relax.

I wish I could tell you I felt happy for her, but I didn't. My mother never acknowledged how she had behaved in those previous nightmarish years. At most, she would say, "Oh, that Dexedrine used to make me nervous."

So this was my mother, Florence, who walked into Salzo's Deli in downtown Pittsburgh on an idyllic spring day in 1984 and began to flirt with the handsome older man who was waiting for his lunch. She'd been helping out at my sister Gloria's hair salon and was picking up their take-out food. The man was in Pittsburgh for a rare city day. He flirted back and said, "If you meet me here next Thursday, I'll buy you lunch."

My mother accepted his offer, and they met the next week. Over corned beef sandwiches and coleslaw, she told him she was a widow with five grown children and she loved movies and dancing even though her knees were bad. He told her he lived on a farm, had been married once, and had lived outside Pittsburgh for a long time. It was the first of many dates.

Later I realized how unusual that must have been for Donald, who rarely spoke to strangers. Florence was just the opposite; she was outgoing and loved to talk. A tiny woman, less than five feet tall, with dark hair and gray-blue eyes, my mother was handsome and energetic.

Donald was five feet, eight inches tall, with gray hair cut close on the sides and swept back on top. He had the erect posture that hinted at a military career, and he was lean. Donald looked like a man whose only mirror was probably a small square over the bathroom sink; he was clean-shaven and neat, but there was little style.

The first time I saw Donald he was dressed up. It was my niece's birthday. We were all dressed casually, but Donald was wearing a business suit. I remember thinking, *Well, he's trying to make a nice impression.* I was amused he was dressing up to meet his girlfriend's family. But I did notice that his white shirt looked as if he had ironed it himself, and his tie was wide with an abstract design, the kind that fills the racks at thrift stores. His shoes were black military brogues, and they were spit-shined.

I made the correct guess that if this relationship continued, I'd see Donald in new clothes. My mother had strong ideas about how people should dress. I'd spent my first twenty years without ever wearing a garment—not even pajamas—with horizontal stripes. "You're too short, and stripes make you look fat," my mother would tell me. So I knew she would have a say in Donald's attire.

As their relationship progressed, Donald's wardrobe did change, but so did my mother's. After she'd visited Donald's farm a few times, my mother asked me where she could buy a "country jacket." I laughed when she said she wanted something similar to the one I wore for backpacking. Next she wanted to know where to get boots that "are good for mud." I gave her an L.L.Bean catalog, which would fit all her needs. My mother was happy, and I was happy for her.

My mother kept her city apartment in downtown Pittsburgh, and Donald had his country place about an hour away. He came into the city for movies, dinner, and opera. She spent weekends at his farm. They laughed a lot. When I came to visit once a month, they seemed happy and affectionate.

When I called her on Sunday mornings—now I was the one who had to call—she often said, "We're still in bed," and the lightness in her voice told me it was not only arthritis keeping Donald and Florence under the covers.

One day I asked cautiously, "You and Donald are having fun?"

"He has to do it every day," she said matter-of-factly. I was speechless. I was in my thirties, and my mother's sex life was better than mine.

"I never knew what it was like, you know," she went on. "When I was married to your daddy, we were just making babies and fixing up that old house. I just never knew about this."

Clearly my mother was finding the way of sex and the single girl as a sixty-nine-year-old gal. But her single status was short-lived.

CHAPTER TWO

Getting to Know Donald

My mother and Donald dated for six months before he proposed. They had romance, companionship, and great fun. He brought her flowers, and she gave him books. When I came to visit, he'd always have a little gift for me too: a little figurine from the Hallmark store or a box of chocolates—and newspaper clippings. My mother and Donald loved to clip articles from the newspapers for family and friends.

But there were things about Donald that did give me pause. I had moved from Washington, DC, to Baltimore by then, and, when I talked to my brothers, they would tell me about some things they noticed about Donald. Sometimes we worried, but mostly we laughed.

One of the things they told me about Donald was that he had a television show he had to watch every evening at five o'clock. He was, we joked, like the character played by Dustin Hoffman in the movie *Rain Man* who always had to be home to watch *Jeopardy!*.

One weekend Donald had made a big fuss when he and my mother were having dinner at Larry's house. Donald was insisting that he had to get home by five o'clock to watch his television show.

"He was going crazy, yelling at Mum that they had to leave 'now, now, now,'" Larry told me.

I thought that was amusing. For years my mother had religiously watched what she called "her stories," and now she was dating a man who had "his stories," too. I thought it was odd—kind of old-guy odd.

But they were dating, and my mother was happy and laughed often. When I'd visit them, Donald was always very polite, and I could see how dear he was with my mother, getting her coffee or holding doors—an old-fashioned kind of man. So I wasn't unhappy or surprised when she told me they were getting married.

Before he proposed to her, Donald had told my mother about his first marriage and where he had lived for so long. But my mother, fearing her children's reaction, waited until after their honeymoon to tell us.

What I learned from my mother was that Donald had been a Marine in China in 1937. He'd gone there with a battalion of United States Marines to protect American interests when Japan was pushing into China. In his first month, the Japanese had begun bombing Shanghai. Donald was part of the Marine battalion protecting the International Settlement and Chinese civilians. He'd had a difficult time in China, but after his release, Donald had come home to his small Pennsylvania hometown, gone back to work, taken more college classes, and married his high school sweetheart.

But one day, my mother said, Donald came home from work in a state of despair, and he shot his mother-in-law and then his wife. My mother was very clear that he'd done an awful thing, but that it was a long time ago, and he was a different man now. Donald was the man she loved, and she asked us only to accept him.

I saw sweetness between my mother and Donald that I'd never seen between my parents. They touched a lot. She'd rub his shoulder or stroke his arm when they watched television, and they always kissed hello and goodbye.

Part of me thought my mother was crazy to marry a man who had killed two people. But another part of me admired my mother for being able to accept him. When she said, "The past is the past," she meant it. She had seen her children through business failures, bad relationships, and divorces. Now we were going to judge her?

But over time Donald's story changed. From him, and from my mother, I would learn more pieces of his story. But it was years later—only after his death—that I began to find Donald's true story. After Donald died, I wanted to know what had contributed to the tragedies in his life and how he survived them. I have spent twenty-five years researching, traveling, and digging into the past so I could understand what happened to Donald Watkins, and I have sifted through all of that to decipher what his story means to all of us.

I feel as if I am sitting on a pivot point when I talk about Donald. I look in one direction and see a totally crazy person—a man who killed two women. But I can also look in the other direction and see Donald as the mental health community did: a person with an illness, a refugee of deinstitutionalization, a man worthy of rejoining society, and ultimately a person who suffered. I worked in human services for many years and know the devastation experienced by people who have been institutionalized in the past.

But then, I look at what is nearby, and I see something else that is troubling. While I see Donald struggling to fit in, suffering with stigma and his own history, I also see my mother marrying him.

As I have lived through and after Donald, this is what I come back to: Yes, he was both gentle and odd, mentally ill, damaged by trauma, and a murderer. But the bottom line is that my mother married him. So I keep asking, "Just who was crazy?"

Once, when Donald was still my mother's boyfriend, I got to see the behavior my brothers talked about. We were out to dinner and halfway through the meal Donald began asking what time it was. Each time one of us tried to answer, my mother would shush us and tell Donald the wrong time. I knew my mother was lying, but I assumed it was because she wanted to stay out later and have more time with her kids.

But when the waitress came to the table with coffee, Donald abruptly demanded to know the time. She said it was almost five o'clock, and I saw panic cross Donald's and my mother's faces at the same time. I knew immediately this was not about how much time to spend at dinner.

Donald nearly toppled my brothers as he pushed his way out of the booth. He stood, looked around, and headed toward the bar at the far end of the restaurant.

My mother turned to Larry and said, "Let him go; he can watch his show in there."

"What's going on?" I asked my mother.

Her reply was noncommittal. "Donald doesn't like to miss his television show."

This, as I came to understand, was an understatement. When we finished eating, we found Donald sitting quietly at one end of the bar, drinking coffee. The bartender, busying himself at the other end of the bar, seemed relieved that we had come to collect this strange customer.

Donald's show was the 1970s syndicated wartime drama *Black Sheep Squadron*. On one level it made sense that Donald liked a television show about bombers in the Pacific, but until Donald met my mother, he didn't have a television. So how did this show get locked and loaded in his psyche?

Another peek into Donald's strange interior came when I heard from my brother Larry about an incident he'd had with Donald at a local mall. Donald and Larry were sitting outside a store while my mother shopped; they were talking and sharing a newspaper. But then, Larry told me, they saw a young Asian family, with their toddler in a stroller, coming down the mall toward them.

Suddenly Donald jumped up and began to scream, "Baby killers, goddamn Jap baby killers."

The young couple were stunned, Larry said. They spun around and sped in the other direction with their child. Larry was mortified.

Later, when he told me about that incident, Larry said, "Di, I don't even think they were Japanese."

Then, one day, my own life was in Donald's hands.

On a fall weekend, I had gone to Pittsburgh to visit my mother and Donald, and we decided to take a drive to Ambridge, Pennsylvania, for shopping and lunch. On this trip, I was showing off my new car and wanted to drive. I knew Donald hated highways, and he refused to drive on them. When he and my mother took trips to Lake Erie or to West Virginia, they drove on back roads going thirty miles per hour—all the way. I chalked this up to Donald's age. As with other elderly people, his diminishing eyesight made three lanes of traffic hard to negotiate. And I knew Donald's reaction time was off; he had difficulty backing out of the driveway at their apartment complex. Larry and I laughed that Donald never heard other drivers honking at him. So, that day, I drove us along narrow back roads all the way to Ambridge, making a one-hour trip take three.

We had our lunch, but shopping took longer than expected. When it was time to go home, I didn't want to drive the long way and suggested we take the highway. I was the driver, after all, so what was the big deal? We argued in the parking lot of a shopping center. Donald refused to get in the car if I was going to drive on the highway.

"He's afraid I can't drive just because he can't," I reasoned, so to get him in the car I said, "Okay, I'll take back roads."

I was sure he'd see that I could manage the highway traffic, and then he'd relax. My mother, with her bad knees, needed to sit up front, so Donald sat in the backseat behind me. And off we went.

One hundred yards up the road, I entered the highway ramp and heard Donald howl from the backseat. Again I assumed he was afraid of my driving, so I said, "Don't worry, I'll get us home," as I accelerated.

My merging speed was up to almost fifty miles per hour when Donald lurched over me from the backseat and grabbed the steering wheel. His body forced my head into my chest, and my field of vision was completely blocked. Suddenly I was wrestling Donald for control of the car. I didn't know if I should brake or how to steer. I had no idea where other cars were. And I knew I was going to die.

I made a conscious decision to minimize the damage and blindly swerved to the right where I hoped there would be a guardrail or shoulder. I was howling and so was Donald. I steered right hard, braked, and hoped I was stopping on something safe and out of traffic. I heard horns blaring and brakes screeching all around me. When my car came to a stop, Donald instantly sat back in his seat as if he had just picked up his hat from the floor.

I was still screaming, flooded with adrenaline, terror coursing through me. My sobs began as I realized it was over. I got out of the car and began to run wildly up and down the shoulder of the road. My mother and Donald sat in the car. I came back and yanked open my mother's door and began to scream at her.

"He's nuts, do you know that? He's insane, he's crazy, he tried to kill us; do you get it? He's nuts; he's just nuts."

And there I was, a raging, sobbing, hysterical woman, racing around in public and screaming at two elderly people who were calmly sitting in the car.

Later, I tried to imagine what being in the backseat had triggered for a man who had been in warlike conditions and then been restrained. Had I naively stepped in front of the train—of Donald's past and pain? But that understanding didn't remove my own rage and my absolute recognition that Donald would have killed—all of us—again.

CHAPTER THREE

Out of Order

I am telling you this story out of order, and that is because Donald was out of order, my mother was out of order, and yes, I'm out of order, too—most people with trauma are. But it's also because I learned Donald's story out of order: First I learned about the ending—the murder. And then I learned about the beginning, which was China. And then I learned some of the middle, and I had to back up and start all over to put the pieces of Donald together again.

Donald was sad and then heroic. He was scary but also admirable. He had been terribly violent, and terrible violence had happened to him as well.

What I did not know when I first met him was that Donald's life was severely out of order. I ache when I think of all the ways he had been traumatized: childhood poverty, a foster home, the Marines, the Japanese in China, St. Elizabeths, the murders, Farview, and afterward, too. But he had no words for any of it, and the people around him were also without words.

Words matter. Words help us make meaning out of experience; they give us something to hold onto. If we had

had the term "post-traumatic stress disorder (PTSD)" in earlier wars, those soldiers might have had something to hold onto. But there was no post-traumatic stress disorder in 1937 or 1945—not even in 1969.

We forget that PTSD was not named as such in Vietnam—not even when our Vietnam veterans started coming home. It wasn't until 1972 when psychologist Chaim Shatan wrote an op-ed piece for *The New York Times* and used the term "Post-Vietnam Syndrome" that people started to take notice. And it took another eight years for post-traumatic stress disorder to become an official diagnosis, five years after the Vietnam War officially ended.

A diagnosis can be a gift. Sometimes people with a mental illness say they don't want to be labeled; they don't want to be "in the system" and they don't want to be identified as mentally ill. There are good reasons: stigma, fear, and often shame accompany a diagnosis.

But it can help enormously when you have words—when you can put a name to feelings and behaviors and thoughts. Say you come home from war and you are happy to be home and proud of your service, but then you notice you are jumpy, feel scared, and see danger everywhere and don't know why; you can think you are insane. You don't understand why you can't go to the mall, take your kids to a movie, or make love to your wife. You just feel bad—bad about yourself—and it is a horrible and ruined kind of bad. But maybe if someone hears your list of symptoms and tells you that you are having this bad time because you have a disease, then you have a starting place. But until then you are out of order: you are broken and in disrepair.

It is important to think about what a diagnosis is. A mental illness diagnosis can sound scientific or definitive, but it is an outcome of language—of language and politics and even economics, as we'll see later. This is especially true with military mental illness. Military trauma, with its many synonyms, shows us how language shifts and adapts to culture, and so what we believe and how we react to "bad behavior" shifts as well.

When I went looking for Donald's story, I met veterans whom no one had talked to about their war experiences. They were men who had been both cruel and kind. They could be hard on people around them, but they were gentle with each other. They ran businesses, sold cars, and taught school. They were war heroes. I met Frenchy and Bones who cared about Donald, and Cliff Wells and George Howe who never judged him.

My mother loved Donald. When my brothers first learned his story, they were furious and wanted him out of my mother's life. But over time, they came to care for this odd man who had joined our family.

And me? I liked Donald when I met him. He was quiet, polite, and kind, and in truth, I was glad my mother had someone to focus on, someone who would take care of her and give me some relief. But I had my own craziness. I didn't escape the trauma of my mother's addiction, and it caught up with me. It affected my thinking, my self-image, and my relationships. When I was thirty, I tried to kill a tree. I was so jealous of my first husband's ex-wife that I tried to kill the tree they'd planted as newlyweds by watering it with bleach every day. The tree kept on blooming. I didn't.

While I looked fairly good on the outside, my insides were filled with constant anxiety, and I had plenty of secret ways to manage all that pain. Just like Donald, I had no words for what was wrong with me, so the "home remedies" I used to "treat" my trauma were alcohol, food, and overwork. Then, feeling bad about that, I piled shame on top of shame.

Trauma expert Bessel van der Kolk talks about trauma as pieces of residue that get stuck in the body and brain. "There is no narrative," he says, "only pieces." The very nature of trauma, according to van der Kolk, is that inside us there are these pieces, and they are all out of order.

But for Donald, a way to have a sense of order meant joining the Marines. The United States Marine Corps is one place where taking orders and keeping order are a way of life.

CHAPTER FOUR

For God and Country

Donald was a Marine. He was a Marine decades ago in China, and he was still a Marine fifty years later in Pennsylvania. Though he was on active duty for only three years, it was true: "Once a Marine, always a Marine."

I was familiar with that saying, but it took me some time to catch on to what this meant. Thankfully, early in my process of researching Donald and asking how to meet ex-Marines, another Marine tipped me off that I should refer to Donald as a *former* Marine; there are no ex-Marines. It would seem that you can be discharged from all of the military services for a myriad of reasons, but you never stop being a Marine.

"We stole the eagle from the Air Force, the anchor from the Navy, the rope from the Army, and on the seventh day when God rested, we overran His perimeter and stole the globe. And have been protecting our shores ever since." This is just one of the many sayings that suggest the special regard Marines hold for themselves. Marines are aggressive, proud, and loyal; Marines are first in and last out; Marines never leave their dead; they have a code of conduct; esprit de corps is Marine culture.

In basic training, Marines are taught that "The US Army is chickenshit in combat, the Navy is worse, and the Air Force is barely even on our side." Marines alone among the military services bestow their name on their enlisted ranks. The Army has officers and soldiers, the Navy has naval officers and sailors, and the Air Force has Air Force officers and airmen—but the Marines have only Marines.

It doesn't take much to draw a line from Donald's Marine duty in China and the prewar days in Shanghai through the Rape of Nanking and then home to Western Pennsylvania and a double murder. If Donald's story happened today, we'd be more sympathetic and maybe say, "Well, that's a tragedy, yes, but he's a vet."

But that's today, and that's how we see things through a lens colored by history. For Americans, World War II was heroic and successful. It was a war with fighting on two fronts: Europe and Asia. We loved our boys who served their country and did their duty. True, a number of them were never quite okay again, but we didn't talk about that much. Our understanding of, and sympathy for, battle fatigue and war neurosis evolved over the course of America's military history.

The other layer of my understanding why there are no ex-Marines came into full focus as I began to correspond with other men who had been in China with Donald. I started my search by subscribing to the magazines *Marine Corps Gazette* and *Leatherneck*. I laugh now when I think about what my mail carrier must have thought as *Leatherneck* began to arrive along with my subscription to *Vogue*. But I also worried whether my liberal judgments could flex enough so I could understand what it means to be a Marine.

Marine training is about learning to follow orders. Marine training also means working as a unit. Being able to respond without thinking is a tool that can save lives. Marines are strong and proud, and yet, paradoxically, they submerge themselves in unity.

Basic training in the Marine Corps is tough and is designed to break men down in order to rebuild them as fighting units. The goal of boot camp is to erase individuality so that recruits will function as a unit. The message to recruits who are becoming Marines is "You are not alone—you are no good alone." And the celebratory message to those who make it is "Now you are a Marine; you can go anywhere, fight anyone, and survive anything."

Aboard the USS *Chaumont* Heading to China—1937

His heart was pounding. The men around him were laughing, swearing, and teasing. There was friendliness among the men. He could see it, but it seemed very far away. It made no sense. They were pushed together—barely an inch between him and the man lying above him. He opened his eyes, and above his face was the curve of a man's buttocks making the canvas curve down toward him. His eyes shifted left, and quickly he closed them again. Another man was next to him, and then more men beyond him.

He's trapped. Trapped. Trapped. He took a deep breath. *I'm all right,* he told himself, *I'm all right; we're just on a ship, going to bed, just gonna sleep soon, real soon, I'll sleep, then it will be okay.* The smells roiled in the cabin—sweat, urine, and shit—so he turned his head. The canvas under him smelled of old vomit. His stomach lurched.

I'm on the ocean, at sea, going to sea, this is big, good, big. The words were not helping. He tried to pray. *God, Father, oh Father in heaven.* He couldn't remember the words, and his heart beat faster. Tight, he felt tight. He pressed his closed eyes tighter, but he could feel the men all around him. They were close, too close.

Out . . . out . . . out. The word started to drum in his head. *I can't,* he thought to himself, *I can't. Gotta do this, can't see me run, can't run, be okay,* but the other word was louder and faster in his head now. *Out, out, out.*

He was afraid to move, afraid to turn; if he shifted he'd be sick or maybe he'd run. *Can't run, no legs to run.* The thought scared him. Even if he got up, he didn't know how to get out. So many men there, canvas beds and duffle bags hung everywhere. *Where is the door? What is it called, the door thing you come through to get in this room?* It wasn't a room, too many men.

Hot, smell of sweat. Vomit smell again.

A man farted loudly, others laughed, then a man belched, more laughter. *It's okay,* he said to himself, *nice guys, good guys.* The man under him turned, and an arm, elbow, or leg thrust into his back. *We are lying on each other like we're dead,* he thought, and the panic rose again. His throat was closing. Breathing was hard, hardly any air. He was so hot; sweat dripped from his face, and he felt the sweat roll down his neck.

A man made a crude joke about a woman. *Bastard,* he thought. Did he say that out loud? He couldn't tell. "Damn," another man said. "My fucking back."

The word was in his head again. *Out.* This time he couldn't stop; he turned. He sat up and hit his head on the bottom of the man above him. "What the fuck, Watkins," the man above said. His leg was over the side. "Don't fucking have to piss now, man, come on," the underneath man said angrily. He had one leg almost to the floor. He stepped on the edge of the canvas bed of the man below him. His foot slid loose, and he fell left into the two men across. "Oh, for Christ's sake, piss in your bed," one man said. He couldn't hear now; he couldn't breathe; he squeezed sideways between the rows of canvas swings with bodies crowded into them. *Out, out, out,* repeated in his head. *Is the door this way?* He stopped. He didn't know, didn't remember, how the ship worked and how they got there.

"The other way, fuckhead," a man lying next to his face snarled into him. He swiveled his head. "The other way. Way out. Out." Then sliding, squeezing, and sliding sideways, he saw the opening. *Head down, duck head.* He missed and scraped the top of his head on the metal frame of the opening. Out to a corridor. *Now where? Head toward the lights.* Breath came now in gulps, and vomit was in his throat. A ladder. *Squeeze. Up the ladder. Now where?* Another ladder ahead. *Up the ladder, cooler air now, air ahead.* Then he was out, up and out onto the deck.

Cool air hit his face. He was still moving fast, too fast. He tripped and went down on one knee. Cool night air fell on him. He breathed. Tears came to his eyes.

"Hey, Marine. New to sea?" A voice from his left. He kept his head down and bit hard to stop his tears. "Too fucking hot for ya? Then sleep on the deck, man; it's the only way to do it."

He looked around now. He could hear again. He heard the man's voice and a bigger sound. Something was roaring outside of him. Huge, louder, fast, shuddering. It was the water, the water and the ship; the ship was cutting through water. He was at sea.

★ ★ ★

I placed small ads in the *Marine Corps Gazette* and *Leatherneck*. The ad said that I was trying to locate Marines who served in China between 1937 and 1940. I gave my home address, phone number, and email address in hopes there might be someone who could help me learn more about the United States Marines in China. I expected to hear from family members who had a father's scrapbook or maybe had an uncle's letters. I was unprepared for what happened.

The first ad appeared in September of 2000, and I began to be drawn into the China Marine world immediately. I came home from work that day, and my message machine flashed, showing I had seven messages. That was a lot for our house, so I grabbed a pen to jot down numbers, but when I heard the first message I couldn't write at all.

A firm male voice said, "Ms. Cameron, this is Staff Sergeant Clifford Wells. I am responding to your notice in the *Marine Corps Gazette*. I believe I can assist you. I served in China 1938 and departed Shanghai on 23 March 1940. Please call me."

He relayed his phone number—I was sure this person was saluting as he spoke—and then he said, "Now I usually bowl on Monday and Wednesday, so it's best to call me on Friday."

I knew no matter how young he had been in 1938, this was a really old guy who sounded like he was still Staff Sergeant Wells.

That week I had more messages like that, delivered in the clipped tones of radio bulletins. And I received letters, which echoed the phone calls: "Dear Ms. Cameron, I am writing in response to your recent notice in the *Marine Corps Gazette*. I believe that I may be able to help you. I am . . ." Then they gave rank, name, duty assignment, and location in China, which always included the full date of arrival and departure.

The letters described each Marine's assignments, duties, and special services rendered: chauffeur to the commander, chef for enlisted men, engineer, or corpsman. Somewhere near the end of each letter the writer would tell me his current age—eighty-six, eighty-seven, eighty-eight, eighty-nine—and how best to contact him. The closings were poignant: "I am happy to help you learn more, but please don't call. I am extremely deaf." Or "I will write back to you again but only when my son comes on Thursday to help me with the mail."

But there was another face of former Marines: emails. The ghosts of China came to me through the Internet. The emails were slightly less formal: "Hi Diane. Rcvd yur email msg. My tour of duty in Shanghai was 3 Nov. 1938 thru 18 May 1940.

Fourth Marines regimental Hdqtrs. I was C.W. radio operator. I have some phone books of Shanghai . . ."

And with each new contact, I received a writer's gift: Each man had documents. Some had scrapbooks or copies of the *Walla Walla*, a weekly newspaper first published by the Marines in Shanghai in 1928. Some men had saved the 1938 Thanksgiving dinner programs that included the menu, and others had box scores of Chinese baseball games with the rosters of players. And they wanted to send it all to me.

Cliff Wells, Frenchy Dupont, and George Howe, along with other former Marines, became my friends and teachers. Despite their age and ailments, they were generous with their time. George, who served with Donald and was now eighty-seven years old, was completely deaf but still wrote to me every week.

These men told me what it was like to be young and far from home, see death all around them, and then have to kill. These men, older than the Greatest Generation, shared that group's reluctance to talk to family about what they'd experienced, but they were willing, almost waiting, to tell me. It was Cliff who asked me one day, "Diane, do you understand what 'hand-to-hand combat' really means?"

I hesitated, knowing in that moment my notion of combat—based on movies—was about to change. And then Cliff told me in gruesome detail.

Frenchy explained what starvation felt like and described his panic and fear when, as a prisoner of the Japanese, he realized he was going blind. And a man nicknamed Bones—because he weighed sixty-three pounds as a prisoner of war (POW)—told me about the strain of being surrounded by violence every day. And it was George who described seeing a guy "go off his rocker" when I asked what it was like to handle dead bodies every day.

It did make me wonder, as it has since my journey began, *Why has no one uncovered this group of men who could write the real*

"We Were There" story of events leading up to World War II? From the urgency I felt from these strangers, pushing to get these materials into my hands, there weren't many people in their lives—not at their own Thanksgiving dinners or at the bowling alley—who were willing to listen. Here were the men who saw the Rape of Nanking and the bombing of the USS *Panay,* who lived the high life of Shanghai—"Paris of the Orient"—and the lowest of lows as prisoners in Bataan and Palawan, and survived. These men, who had been through all of that and still identified themselves first and always as United States Marines, wanted to tell their stories.

I am aware of the ease with which the phrase "China Marine" rolls from my tongue now. The stories led to facts, and the giant puzzle started to fill in. I know Donald and the Marines were transported on the USS *Chaumont,* "up north" means Tientsin, and "guard duty" means confronting the Japanese. I know "bombing detail" means picking up body parts all day and that we were at war with Japan long before Pearl Harbor.

America tried to avoid war with Japan in those years, but war pressed closer. There had been American business interests in China for thirty years; Standard Oil had a large operation there, as did a dozen other American companies. The International Settlement was a kind of neutral zone, and there was an American embassy in Peiping (later called Peking, then Beijing). The American businesses had thousands of employees in Shanghai, Nanking, and the surrounding area. In the 1930s Japan began to push against the Chinese, and the Americans and other foreign nationals were in the middle but trying, ever so delicately, to stay neutral.

Franklin D. Roosevelt's administration was basically pro-Chinese and anti-Japanese but struggled to restrain the Japanese without actually fighting. But the Japanese pushed hard against the Americans, which led to the delicate duty of the United

States China Marines who had no orders to intervene; they were only to protect Americans and American business interests. However, in 1937 their diplomatic position became more tenuous. In December of that year, Japanese aircraft bombed the USS *Panay*, an American gunboat sitting in harbor. It was a hostile gauntlet thrown down by the Japanese, but President Roosevelt, unprepared for war, accepted Japan's explanation that the daytime bombing was an accident. Instead of military retribution the United States asked Japan for monetary compensation, but the China Marines knew that war had moved closer and their lives were going to get worse.

"I remember when the *Panay* was bombed," Cliff told me. "We were alerted that morning, and we locked and loaded; we'd always drilled and had emergency drills; you couldn't see all those bodies everywhere and not know this was a war. We were on alert; we heard the *Panay* went down and were ready to march into the Japs. We were on our way to confront them with arms but then got word to step down. Washington said, 'It was an accident.' But nobody in China thought it was an accident. It was the middle of the day, and the *Panay* was flying her colors. They shot at our ship, and we just sat there."

Donald's discharge papers say that he "participated in the defense of the International Settlement, Shanghai, China." It sounds romantic. And it certainly was international. The International Settlement was a rich, extravagant, highly scented, and scenic place. People from at least twenty different countries lived there, including British, French, Dutch, and American civilians, and there were concessions—business districts—operated by the French and the Japanese.

"How ya gonna keep 'em down on the farm after they've seen Paree?" the wartime song asks. Shanghai was Paris on steroids, and the Marines were young and green. I can picture the nightclubs, shows, and rustling silks; the jewelry, necklaces, beads, and women all for sale. I can hear the ice tinkling in glasses and the music: Chinese musicians on the streets and jazz and classical music coming from the clubs at all hours. When I try to look through Donald's twenty-two-year-old eyes, I wonder at all he saw.

China duty had the reputation of being the envy of the military services in those few years before World War II. It was considered light duty—Monday through Friday 10:00 a.m. until 4:00 p.m.—and the excellent exchange rate meant young men with low salaries could gamble and party, buying all the booze, silk, Chinese goods, and women they wanted. Back at the barracks a houseboy was spit-shining their shoes and tidying the bunks to dime-spinning Marine standards.

But there was a dark side to this life. For those who know what happened there in 1937 and 1938, "International Settlement" was also code for horrors beyond belief.

Over the years, photos of the torture and killing have been published and exhibited. In 1994 *The Rape of Nanking* by Iris Chang described what the Japanese did to Chinese civilians. The atrocities were concentrated in Nanking but spread through all of occupied China and into the domain of the Marines. More than 300,000 Chinese civilians were murdered. But it was worse than murder; first they were tortured and mutilated, then killed.

In the 1930s there were bubblegum cards sold in the United States that showed pictures of the more discreet scenes of dead and decapitated bodies in China. This was, of course, our own anti-Japanese propaganda, but the pictures were a small sample of the atrocities Iris Chang would later uncover from photos and eyewitness accounts—men, women, and children brutally raped, tortured, and coldly used for bayonet practice. Chinese civilians were chopped, slashed, cut, and pulled to pieces.

One of the most sadistic games of Japanese soldiers was capturing pregnant Chinese women, placing bets on the gender of the fetus, and then cutting open the woman's abdomen to determine a winner. The fetus would be pulled from the woman's belly, tossed in the air, and caught on a Japanese soldier's bayonet. The mother would be left to bleed to death. Sometimes the Japanese soldiers might cut off a woman's hands or feet and insert them in her genitals. And our China Marines stood as witnesses.

This torture did not last for only a day or a week; it continued for months. Our Marines, assigned to protect only the International Settlement, could witness these atrocities but not interfere. Every day as they patrolled the International Settlement and the perimeter of Shanghai, and later as they traveled north to Tientsin, the Marines saw bodies everywhere: men with no genitals or with severed penises stuffed in dead mouths and dead women with fetuses dangling from sliced bellies, bottles and sticks in vaginas, and headless bodies strewn on streets, along roads, and in doorways. Witnesses—missionaries and soldiers who recorded their accounts—said that the dogs in the Chinese villages waddled because they were so bloated from their constant diet of human flesh.

As I digest the horror of what Donald saw in China, I have a recurring thought: *Murder by shooting begins to seem so refined, so decent, and almost sane.* And as the pieces of Donald's story came to me and I met his peers from China, I wondered, *What happens to a person who saw all of that, the dancers and the death, the music and the mutilation? What happens to a man who paid children to clean his room and watched them get beheaded as a game? What happens to men who see women's bodies cut to pieces?*

When I turn and try to look through Marine eyes, it makes me wonder about the other Marines, men like Cliff, Frenchy, and Bones who came back from China to live long civilian lives. *How did they survive? And just who is crazy?*

Donald at the Barracks in Shanghai—1937

He was standing outside the barracks facing the small service road that led to Bubbling Well Road. The day's mandatory drills were done, and he was glad to stand outside and stretch his back and neck. It wasn't a bad day, really, marching; they marched all the time. They were parade ready that way, which was a big part of who they were: the clipped steps, short strides, long steps, changing tempo, the sergeant barking orders, then the rapid steps. They learned in basic how to turn on a dime and not step on the man in front of them. "Keep your focus on the front crease in your pants," he'd learned.

He'd done well today, and he was in great shape on the shooting range; his scores were staying high, so he'd have no trouble qualifying next week. You had to score in the ninetieth percentile to achieve a qualifying score, which allowed you to place out and move on to another level of training. He'd be fine but would take the skill test anyway. That way he'd be able to try and win the extra badge. Nice to have those badges, even though they didn't get you promoted.

"Couldn't hurt, couldn't hurt," he'd told Dante, his friend from New Jersey. "Can't hurt that the higher-ups know your name," as long as it was for doing something good.

He'd learned that back home in the plant. He'd worked as a laborer for years but had pride about it—do it well, do the last detail, clean your work space, and never turn your shift over to the next man until you've swept your box. *It's just what's right.*

He stretched again. Still warm, but they said it could get cold here. He'd been given a fur hat when he arrived, a big fur hat like some Russian would wear. He'd laughed and said, "We going to dress like lady bears?"

"Marine, you'll freeze your ass off here and be glad for the hat."

On the *Chaumont* he'd met some guys who'd been here before, had done China duty and volunteered to come back.

"Best drill you'll find," they told him. "And wait 'til you see the girls."

"And wait 'til they see him and those blue eyes," another man had said. "The Chink girls think blue eyes are special."

"Yeah, and the Russian girls are easy to get something, if you know what I mean."

He did know what the man meant but wasn't so confident. No one knew he was a virgin. He'd seen some women in Pittsburgh at the burlesque house he'd gone to with other boys. They'd all gone to see the stripper, and afterward some guys went to another place and paid ten dollars to have sex.

"Women there will put their mouth on you," one guy told him. "That's not so bad, Watkins, a little sweetness where it counts."

On the ship some men talked about women all the time. He laughed with everyone else, but it made him feel strange. He'd been slapped so much by Mrs. Kiefer if he even looked at the girls in the foster home.

"Don't you ever put your hands on a girl. Don't you ever; do you hear me?" She'd screamed this at him once when she caught him looking at one of the older girls undressing. He hadn't even meant to look. He'd come upstairs, and she was undressing in front of the sink to give herself a wash. He just kept looking when she took off her blouse and he could see her slip and her bosom showing through that.

Dante and the other guys in his unit wanted to go and see the White Russian girls tonight. He'd go along and have some dinner. They'd gone down to the French Concession the first night they got off the ship. They wore their dress blues and received applause from the Chinese people along the roads. "Happy Marines, happy Marines," people called out to them. It didn't sound like they really knew English, but he'd felt proud again like he did the day they left San Diego. People had come out to cheer and wave flags, and they even held their little kids up in the air. He felt like a Marine that day.

Dante and the other two Marines were coming out of the barracks now. "You coming?" they asked.

"Absolutely," he said.

"Hey, Watkins, grab your coat," Dante said, bending near him, untying and then retying his boot. "You'll be cold; go on and get your jacket."—

He nodded and ran back to the barracks and for a moment was alone in the long room with twelve bunks. It was so clean. He'd been part of the cleaning, but he hadn't actually seen it without people. Now he was alone and liked the feeling. The rows of bunk beds lined up just so, each cot looking exactly like the others, and a faint smell of soap, waxy shoe polish, and the fine oil they used on their guns all mixed together. Today they had met these boys, little Chinese kids who came for jobs. The kids would make your bed, shine your shoes, and clean anything, anything except your rifle—you never let anyone else clean your rifle. But for a dime or a quarter a kid would clean your bunk and boots for a week. He laughed.

He walked to his bunk at the end of the row and lifted his short khaki jacket from a hook on the wall. "Marine Corps, yes sir," he said softly to himself.

They walked along until they came to Bubbling Well Road where there were several rickshaw men, kids really, twelve or thirteen maybe, saying, "Get a girl, US, wanna get a girl for you, US?" The other men had grabbed a rickshaw up ahead and waved to him and Dante to come on. They told the man who pulled the cart to go to the Shanghai Bar. The four squeezed into the two short seats, and the man hoisted the bars onto his shoulders, tipping the cart back for balance.

As they rode along Bubbling Well Road, he could see other Marines walking along. They'd call out to the four men, "Get something good!" and when they saw the sailors from the *Chaumont*, also out tonight, they'd give an exaggerated salute and say, "Man overboard" and "Hit the head, sailor."

They crossed into the International Settlement through the large gate near Soochow Creek. A tall fence with barbed wire had been added earlier in the summer. *Like a prison,* he thought. Once inside they paid the rickshaw driver in American change. He asked the others, "How much is that for each?"

"We'll settle up later, Watkins. Just buy a drink or something, okay?"

They had dinner at a small pub, British, his new friends told him. You got roast beef here, not like the slop on the ship, real roast beef. They had beer and ale with dinner, and he noticed a pretty, red-haired woman at the bar smiling. She came to their table with another girl when they were finishing their beer. "You lonely American boys look pretty new; do you know Shanghai? Need any directions?"

Dante beamed at the girls, but the other man said, "Hey, doll, we're looking for a little more tonight. We're just off the ship, you know. We're looking for the mama-san; we need someone nice for our friend here," and gestured to Donald.

"Don't get in trouble, boys." She smiled and walked back to the bar.

"Are those whores?" Dante asked the other men, leaning across the table.

"No, just girls. They'll talk your ear off if you buy them a beer. Nice girls, but you're not gonna get anything from them."

After another beer the other men went off, and Donald and Dante walked around the International Settlement. They got confused several times and ended up in alleys, so they tried to backtrack but got lost again. A couple of times they saw men fighting and some men playing a game with little cups on a table. They could tell it was gambling by the voices and the Chinese money that the men were laying on the ground.

They found their way back to the main street where the pub was and walked back and forth, listening to the music coming out of the bars. Lights flashed overhead. Girls in swanky, satin dresses walked by with soldiers, then several sailors came toward them and started to say, "Hey, the Marines, hey, fucking Marines," then recognized them from the ship and laughed. "Hey, we'll buy you two greens a beer," the sailors said and tried to pull them into a bar.

"Thanks, fellas, but we got early leave, gotta get back to the barracks," Dante said, pulling Donald along.

"Why'd you say that?" Donald asked.

"Sailors have two days to spend a month's pay; they'll get us in trouble, and we'll never get leave again. Just stick with the Marines. Besides, tomorrow we're gonna get clothes. We'll go to the China man store I heard about and get us suits made. We're gonna get navy suits and cashmere topcoats with wide lapels and belts that tie. Bankers in New York don't even have coats like that."

★ ★ ★

I do my research on weekends and travel to see my China Marines or stare at microfiche at the Naval Archives. At home I read everything I can find on trauma and war.

I am reading the book *Soul Repair: Recovering from Moral Injury After War* by Rita Nakashima Brock and Gabriella Lettini. These professors of theology state that moral injury occurs when soldiers look at their behavior in a negative way because they believe they have violated their core moral beliefs. They may have participated in or couldn't stop the killing of people, the torture of prisoners, the abuse of corpses, or the mishandling of human remains. These actions result in the soldiers believing that they live in a meaningless world and have become indecent people, even if what they did was out of their control or justified.

When we look away from the full role our soldiers play, it may be a great denial by our society. Many of our warriors are not only victims of trauma, but they also have been the perpetrators or the ones who permitted some form of revenge during war. Then, when they come home, their shame and our denial collude to deny them safe places to reconcile those actions.

Brock and Lettini tell us that for effective treatment of moral injury, the greater community must participate in healing rituals with our soldiers. But because accepting perpetrators of violence is so much less tolerable than accepting victims of violence, we have not been able to find ways to help our soldiers heal.

I attend the Veterans, Trauma and Treatment conference in Rhinebeck, New York, and listen to an Air Force major and physician speak about moral injury and suicide. She offers this deeply sad statistic: "For every one or two soldiers who die in combat, sixteen will die in suicide." It is her belief that "moral injury—much more than PTSD—is the greater factor in military suicide," and moral transgression causes the greatest injury. No drug can mask that damage, and traditional therapies seem powerless in the face of moral injury.

But when we look at the scattered pieces of trauma in one person's life, we have to remember that it's not as simple as pieces of a jigsaw puzzle lying on a flat surface that might, with therapy and time, be coaxed into place. No, trauma is more of a three-dimensional puzzle with some of the pieces permanently lost. This was true in Donald's story, too.

CHAPTER FIVE

Missing History: Donald's Past Has a Past

The first time I wrote about Donald was in the spring of 1999. I had been writing a column for the Albany *Times Union* newspaper for several years, and I wanted to write about Donald in May because it's Mental Health Month. Donald had died three years before, so it felt like a good time to tell his story.

I wanted to focus on something I had been thinking about for a long time: It was this idea that sometimes people who seem awful or bizarre to us when we read about them in a newspaper often are or were, in many ways, like all of us, human beings who wanted things we all want. The murderer, the serial killer, and the employee who "goes postal" were somebody's uncle or sister, and they had all once been someone's child. But my planned column was to take a hit, and it was that rejection that sent me on this long and amazing search. I was about to learn that there was much more to Donald's story.

I sent the editor my story about Donald and how, though he had had a tragic past, my family had come to love him.

I thought the piece would be provocative and compassionate. But the editor kicked the column back to me with this note: "There's something wrong with your dates. It doesn't add up."

I was annoyed. I knew my family's story, didn't I? But I was also embarrassed; the editor returned the story because she'd done some simple math. I had described Donald as a young Marine recently home from China when he committed the murders, but I had said that he was in his late sixties when he was released from Farview after serving twenty-two years. She was right; it didn't add up. The story as I'd written it would have made Donald older at the time of the murders, but I knew he was twenty-six when he went to China. What was I missing?

I wrote a different piece for the May column and put Donald aside. But it nagged at me, and I decided I had to get more information. I made a call to a newspaper in Washington, Pennsylvania, and asked for archival records, explaining the murder story from the 1950s. The archivist referred me to the town public library, so I called there and gave the approximate dates. The librarian said that if she found anything, I'd have to pay for photocopying. I mailed a brief letter and sent her twenty dollars for expenses.

Two weeks later a thick packet arrived. The librarian had gone through the *Washington Observer* archives and found mention of Donald Watkins in the news of March and May of 1953. She enclosed copies for me.

There were about fifteen pages of photocopied newsprint. The old newspaper layout was busy and cramped, and the photocopies were grainy and blurred. The first article, from March 9, two days after the murders, had this headline: "Murder Charged in Killings." In a sidebar were two grainy photos with a smaller heading: "Victims of Double Slaying Here."

The first photo was captioned "Mrs. Norma Watkins." This was how I learned the name of Donald's first wife, and it was the first time I saw her picture. Norma (Frye) Watkins had a round, pretty face and dark, shoulder-length hair. She was smiling. It looked like an employment photo; she'd been a school nurse.

The next photo was also of a woman, with the caption "Mrs. Catherine Frye," Norma's mother and Donald's mother-in-law. She also had dark hair, but hers was fuller, almost bushy, and she was wearing glasses. She had deep creases running from her nose to her chin, accentuating a down-turned curve of her mouth.

The next day's newspaper had more details. The March 10 clippings from the archive included the obituaries for Norma Watkins and Catherine Frye. There was a separate obituary for each woman, and each stated that friends could visit the Graham P. Cowleson Funeral Home until two o'clock on the afternoon of March 10, when private services would take place.

Then, turning more photocopied pages, I saw another headline: "Watkins Views Body of His Bride." With my interest piqued, I read the following from the news clipping:

> Police in attendance said Watkins, a former schoolteacher and a welder, did not break down during the short visit. He spent all of his time at the bier of his wife, Norma, turning down an invitation to view the body of his other victim, Mrs. Catherine Frye. . . . Watkins spent approximately 15 minutes at the funeral home in one of the strangest crimes of recent years here. Accompanying officers stated that he kissed the remains of the girl, whose life he ended with a fusillade of 10 shots.

I sat back in my chair. I had the actual date of the murders and a description of the "girl whose life he ended," and I had this other thing: the pictures of the two women whom Donald had killed. Their pictures made them more real to me. I also had the bizarre fact that Donald had been permitted to visit the funeral home and had kissed the remains of his dead wife.

The rest of the newspaper clippings revealed more, and some were touching. In reporters' interviews with people who knew him, Donald was described as a "favorite teacher" and "the best worker ever." Howard Patterson, Donald's boss at the Washington Tool and Machine Company, said, "I feel sorry for him. As far as we were concerned around the plant, he was a smart fellow and a mighty good, hard worker." Another of Donald's employers, "a veteran official at the Disco Machine Plant," said,

> I've had more than half-dozen youngsters go to college while they were working here, but if there was one who seemed sure to get somewhere because of his ambition, ability to work, and intelligence, it was Don Watkins. Then, referring to the crime, he shook his head. I just can't understand it.

Also in the account was this statement: "One Disco employee who said his son attended the Robinson Township School said the students there thought a great deal of Watkins as a teacher. He had formed a boys' club."

There were more comments from coworkers and neighbors who praised Donald as a "good neighbor," and one who said that Donald had "no family in the world." He was described as an orphan and a foster child.

The people quoted all made Donald's past more real to me. It wasn't only my mother's story. These clippings showed me that I didn't know Donald's entire story. He had been a teacher and a welder. His wife was a nurse, not a teacher, and they had been married only seven months at the time of the killings. So what happened? How did he get from China to this tragedy?

There was more. As I turned the pages of the old newspaper clippings, I found another startling fact: The headline from Thursday, March 12, 1953, said, "Watkins in Mental Hospital Seven Years." What? What was this? Donald had been in a mental hospital before the murders? Then I read the lead paragraph:

> The strange story of Donald K. Watkins, slayer of his wife and mother-in-law in a fusillade of gun fire Saturday afternoon, reached a new climax yesterday with the revelation that Watkins spent seven years of his adult life in a mental hospital.

What I learned from those clippings was that the then district attorney Ray Zelt, when pressed to account for the killings, went looking for and discovered Donald's military past. Most people in Washington County, and perhaps his wife, too, assumed that when Donald returned home in 1946, he was returning directly from the war. He had gone to China, that was known, and he was a Marine, but what was now revealed was that after spending three years in the service, Donald came home not to the town of Washington, Pennsylvania, but to St. Elizabeths Hospital in Washington, DC. The March 12, 1953, *Washington Observer* story provided the details:

> He apparently kept successfully hidden from all except a handful of people the fact that he spent seven years in a mental institution. The first solid thread of Watkins's life is picked up when he went to work for the Disco operation of the Pittsburgh Consolidated Coal Company in 1935 at the age of 23. He worked there less than a year but so impressed his supervisors with his ability and willingness to work that they still recall it vividly.
>
> In 1936, he enlisted in the Marines. The only reason fellow workers can give for that action

is that Watkins thought it would be a glamorous adventure. He served in China during that enlistment and just what happened in that period to Watkins is apparently not known, but three years later he was an inmate in a mental institution in Washington, DC.

So Donald's past had a past, and a new chronology emerged. And now I had more questions. I had to find out what had happened to Donald in China.

Friends and Factories: Donald in Tientsin— A China Marine

Donald was assigned to the 6th Marines, which in early 1938 was divided into two sections. One half of the battalion returned to the United States, and the other half was sent north to Tientsin. Donald, along with his good friends Dante Caruso and George Howe, traveled through the Grand Canal and up the Yangtze and Yellow Rivers on United States Navy boats to take on their new duties in Tientsin.

Tientsin was a different kind of Chinese city than what the Marines had seen. They had visited Peiping, with its ancient ruins, pagodas, and temples, and they had loved the bustle of Shanghai, which was modern and quite international. Tientsin, on the other hand, was an industrial city and a center for textiles, chemicals, and iron and steel production. There were several colleges in Tientsin and a major university. This northern city would have felt familiar to Donald, who had grown up in Western Pennsylvania's coal and steel region.

In Tientsin the Marines had their usual military routines, but there was increased restriction of their outside activities. Japan was actively at war with China now, and the United States was trying to stay out of it. The bombing of the USS *Panay* a few months earlier had been a warning to Americans.

The company commander at Tientsin was Captain Bemis and "the gunny"—chief operations officer—was Gunnery Sergeant Beardin. George Howe told me, "Behind his back we called Beardin 'smartly and audibly,' as that was what he was always saying to us: 'Do everything smartly and audibly.'"

Donald's company lived in a long, single-story, brick building on the east side of Tientsin. The building was an old apartment complex that had been vacated after World War I and was later occupied by the 15th Infantry of the United States Army.

Chinwangtao, just outside the compound, had a beer hall and the "authorized" whorehouse for the Marines. It was considered "authorized" because the girls who provided services to the Marine detachment were regularly examined by military doctors. Their services were for Americans only, and the house was run by a mama-san in cooperation with the United States Marine Corps.

The Marines' primary mission in Tientsin was to provide a visual presence of the American military and to monitor and report on the movement of Japanese troops. These Marines—Donald and his colleagues—also continued their usual duty of collecting, stacking, and burying the bodies and body parts of murdered Chinese civilians.

In Tientsin, Donald and Dante Caruso became regular handball partners. Donald had learned to play as a freshman at Duquesne University in Pittsburgh, and he played several times a week in Shanghai. It was following a regular handball game with his friends that Donald's life began to come apart.

In the letters he sent to me over several years, George Howe helped me to understand Donald's life in Tientsin. On yellow legal-sized paper, George Howe described what happened that specific day in the Marine barracks. Dante and Donald had returned to their room, sweating and tired from their game. Other men, including George, were sitting on bunks enjoying their usual afternoon drink of small bottles of Coca-Cola with whisky added. Upon entering the barracks, Donald was given a drink, "and within seconds, he had gone off his rocker." The other Marines, with Dante helping, restrained Donald and dragged him to the sick bay.

From there, Donald was kept in a "quiet room," which was a padded cell. "Don was so enraged," George recalled. "He pulled the iron-framed door completely out of the cell."

After that, two Marines guarded Donald while he was in the cell. It would be the first of many times Donald would have to be guarded.

CHAPTER SIX

Nuts for the Nation:
St. Elizabeths Hospital

St. Elizabeths Hospital is America's most famous mental institution. Admitting its first patients in 1855, St. Elizabeths was the first federal hospital devoted entirely to the care of the mentally ill. St. Elizabeths served the United States as a military hospital for the insane from the Civil War through Vietnam. What happened to those soldiers, however, and what their conditions were called, has varied widely over those years.

For Americans, World War II was an especially positive and patriotic war. Those supportive feelings about the war accrued to the men who had fought in the war. But we also have to pay attention to the demographics, politics, and economics of World War II. The best way to do that is to back up and consider that war compared to the previous one.

In World War I, the United States was fighting in Europe, and Americans were greatly divided; there was a considerable reluctance about America's entry into the war, so President Woodrow Wilson pledged neutrality. But after the sinking of the *Lusitania* and Germany urging Mexico to declare war against the United States, the decision to join the Allies was made. At that time the United States' population was high, and there was a good supply of young men—enough soldiers to fight in a war.

Because there were enough soldiers, the way they were regarded was different. These young men were, sadly, more disposable. When soldiers in World War I behaved in ways that reflected what we later called "battle fatigue," they were not seen as men who were ill but as having issues of poor character. It was not uncommon in World War I for soldiers to be court-martialed for desertion or treason if they froze in combat or failed on the battlefield. There were even cases in which men had been court-martialed and executed for "noncompliance."

But in World War II, the United States was fighting in both Asia and Europe, and the need for soldiers doubled at the same time that the American population was experiencing a steep decline.

When Pearl Harbor occurred, the United States Navy had 284,427 men in service. This increased to more than 3,380,000 by the war's end. When the war began in Europe, the Army had 189,839 in service, which grew to about 8,270,000 at war's end. And the Marines at the time of Pearl Harbor had 54,359 in their ranks, which grew to 475,000 by 1945. There were similar increases for the Army Air Corps, Coast Guard, and Merchant Marine. In total, more than sixteen million Americans served in World War II.

Given these numbers, the Pentagon faced a critical economic and manpower issue. While in the past soldiers who "broke" could be replaced or discarded, in World War II the United States could not afford to do that.

So the Pentagon began to investigate what could be done for soldiers to prevent breakdowns and quickly return them to the front lines. The government also needed to cope with the increased numbers who were returning home and flooding the military hospitals.

As a result, the Pentagon began to invest in research and new practices for the treatment and prevention of military mental illness. Between 1940 and 1946, the Pentagon invested more than $30 million in psychiatric research to stabilize soldiers and keep them fighting.

That investment spilled over into civilian life. In those years the *Journal of Clinical Psychology* magazine was founded; women's magazines published articles about personal psychology and mental hygiene. Popular books and movies picked up the theme, and Hollywood became a source of education on mental illness.

Mary Jane Ward published her bestselling novel, *The Snake Pit,* in 1946, and in 1948 it became a movie staring Olivia de Havilland and was nominated for six Academy Awards. The film "reads" like a documentary on mental illness and its then-current treatments.

The cultural pendulum was swinging. Was war trauma a mental problem or a physical one? Did it require medical treatment or was it a problem of the mind, best treated by psychotherapy?

Visiting St. Elizabeths Hospital

When I learned that Donald had spent time as a patient at St. Elizabeths Hospital, I wrote to the chief administrative officer and requested a visit. Because of the high security at the hospital, it took almost a year to get permission and an appointment.

On October 13, 2001, I flew to Washington, DC, and then took a taxi to the Anacostia neighborhood. Stepping out of the taxi, alone in front of the grim-looking hospital, and in a part of the nation's capital far from the monuments and museums, I wondered what I was doing here and if I was crazy.

I approached the elderly guard at the end of the driveway and explained that I had an appointment. He directed me to the building ahead where his supervisor would meet me. As

I approached the building, a man emerged and explained that he was both the acting director and the chief horticulturist for the hospital.

As we walked the grounds, I questioned him about his work. "Do you still have patients working on the grounds with you?"

"Yes," he said. "See the red wall there?" He pointed to a high brick wall at the other end of the campus. "That's where the patients are now, you know." He nodded at me. "The famous ones."

"Oh," I said, worrying. He probably thought that's why I was there. So many reporters wanted to write about John Hinckley, now the most famous patient at St. Elizabeths.

He showed me the greenhouse where he led the horticulture therapy program. "I talk a lot about plants and such," he said. "We don't have the budget anymore for many plantings."

History of St. Elizabeths Hospital

Ground was broken for the Government Hospital for the Insane in 1852. It was a "modern" facility that introduced the "moral treatment" of mental illness, which dictated that facilities should provide congenial, even beautiful, natural surroundings for the inmates.

The hospital's name change came about during the Civil War. Because Washington was located so close to actual battle sites of that time, the Government Hospital for the Insane was used to treat battlefield casualties. Civil War wounds were horrendous. The minié ball, ammunition used in guns of that period, shattered bones so completely that limbs could not be set, and most wounded soldiers had their arms and legs amputated on the battlefield. Those who survived the first amputation were brought to the Government Hospital for the Insane to await more surgery.

The Civil War soldiers convalescing there refused to write home saying they were at a hospital for the insane, so they simply told loved ones that they were at St. Elizabeth's Hospital—sometime after the Civil War the apostrophe was dropped from the name.

Donald's Marine Corps records show that he came to St. Elizabeths in a "convoy of insane mental cases" in 1939. Treatments used at that time included "hydrotherapy"—ice-water baths lasting eight hours to induce hypothermic shock. Other "modern" practices were "insulin shock therapy," which consisted of injections of high doses of insulin to cause seizures and coma, and "metrazol-induced convulsions," which were used in an attempt to help with schizophrenia and affective psychoses.

One of the common and tragic "treatments" at St. Elizabeths, which was used in many mental hospitals at that time for patients considered aggressive or hard to manage, was the prefrontal lobotomy. In that procedure a scalpel or sharp pick was inserted through a small hole drilled in the forehead or pushed diagonally through the eye socket and then rotated to sever the tissues connecting the frontal lobes of the brain.

However, the most common treatment was electro-convulsive therapy. Before using it on a patient in 1938, Ugo Cerletti "discovered" electroconvulsive treatment when he observed its use in a slaughterhouse where it was being used to paralyze cattle before they were slaughtered. At hospitals like St. Elizabeths, electroshock was used in single or multiple applications to treat hysteria, schizophrenia, depression, postpartum depression, agitation, catatonia, and, of course, war trauma or "shell shock." Because Donald's diagnosis from China was "dementia praecox," or schizophrenia, there is a high probability that he received shock treatment.

Donald Leaves St. Elizabeths

Once, before his official discharge, Donald "escaped" from St. Elizabeths. In fact, patients there were so heavily medicated that they were allowed to roam the large ungated grounds, so one day Donald walked off the campus and started hitchhiking home to Pennsylvania. He was picked up a few days later and returned to the hospital.

It is likely that Donald's official discharge from St. Elizabeths in 1946 came about for several reasons. World War II was ending, and there was a general sense that all soldiers, even men who had come into hospitals for shell shock, should go home to their families. It's also likely that Donald seemed improved. He was a hard worker, and those good traits, which employers later acknowledged, were also present at St. Elizabeths, where he worked in the laundry and woodworking shops.

Donald's discharge would also have been helpful to the hospital. The population of the hospital was rapidly increasing as more soldiers were returning from the war. Many were soldiers for whom the effect of their war trauma did not reveal itself until after they arrived home. And there were others who, upon being discharged from military medical facilities, were then identified as needing psychiatric care. Frankly, St. Elizabeths needed the beds.

Donald and Ezra Pound at St. Elizabeths—1945

He was standing at the window near the back corner of the South Ward dayroom. He was here now instead of in the other ward because of his "taking leave" a few weeks earlier. He just walked away that day, walked off the grounds, toward the street, and kept walking. He hadn't planned to leave, or "escape," as they called it. He saw the road was there, just a short way below the lawn. Then he found himself on that road and walking with no one behind him, no one following him, no one running after him.

He walked for a couple of miles, and then he was in the city. From there he thought, *Why go back? Just go home.* So he started to thumb a ride.

"Where ya coming from, soldier?" a driver asked him.

"China, went up the Yellow River to Tientsin."

The driver whistled and said, "Holy cow, I bet you seen a lot, huh?" That man drove him all the way to Baltimore and gave him five bucks for dinner. He could be home in Midway, Pennsylvania, in three days.

They put him in solitary when back at the hospital. The "quiet room," they called it. *Ha, nothing quiet about it. Wrapped you in those wet sheets—miserable, can't move at all when you're wet—the Japs should have known about wet sheets.* Then he was in that little room where they slide slop under the door to eat, no dining room for days, with that little window and the lights. *Lights on day and night, and the little window would open and then close real fast, people looking at you all the time—anybody, anybody could look at you.* The doctor, the nurse, even the guy with the mop, they all looked in at him. *Can't even take a piss in privacy.* He figured it out, though. *Just make the best of it, watch them, and figure it out.* He sat still, hung his head, and said "sir" and "ma'am" until they eventually let him out.

He had to talk, though; that was the worst. They would ask, "Donald, will you tell us what feelings made you want to go home?"

There were no feelings, just the field and the road and then the next road. That's what freedom felt like, just a road and you walking.

But he talked, made up things so they'd shut up. He learned it was easier to talk than to get pills or the electric shock. *That was the worst; you'd be dumb and nuts for days after that.* He had that several times in the beginning, day after day of that shock. *It was horrible. The other bastards here, they made them hold you down.* That was the very lowest thing, when they made him hold down some other poor bastard so they could stick that band on the guy's head and make him vomit and drool.

You wouldn't know anything after that, not your name or if you had kids. A man wouldn't know the guy he bummed a cigarette from that morning. They'd go around leaving their dicks hanging out of their pants; it was awful.

No, he figured out that one: *You talk, make things up, and sometimes look sad, never mad. Stay busy, but not too busy.* It helped to watch the others, though. Some of them worked for the hospital and looked like patients, but they were spies and liars. They would tell the nurse if someone beat off or saved up his pills— that would get a person shocked for sure. No, better to watch the other ones, the sicker ones, as they'd sit and stare or play cards by themselves and have the young nursing students ask them, "Wouldn't you like to make some crafts with us today?" *What a pathetic bunch they were to want to work with lunatics. Little whores; they just want to grab our dicks and see what we've got.*

The longest part of the day was from after lunch until dinner. Mornings had the cleaning; a guy could mop, empty trash cans, or fold hot towels in the big laundry. Maybe fix screens or hang a new door. All of that was better than helping in the unit downstairs; that's where they made him hold the bastards down to get shocks. That wasn't right for a man to do to someone else.

But time wore on. There was a bunch of guys over there playing cards, and there, across the way, that other one talking, talking, talking, crazy.

There was a lot of talk today. There was a big fuss downstairs because a big-deal writer was coming in; a poet they said, Ezra Pound. He wrote about birds or lace doilies or something, but they said he was a traitor. He'd gone on the dago radio in Sicily and talked about the American troops, said the president was a liar. *Why the fuck would anyone do that?* He was a bastard liar, but now they said he was nuts.

One of the aides said there'd been a trial to show he was nuts, "Like the rest of you boys, he's a flying fruitcake, so he's coming to live with you."

The aide who was taking away food trays laughed. "Fucking fruit poet, should be shot for treason, but he gets to play with you boys," he said, waving his arm at the dayroom. Some men looked up and then went back to their game of cards.

"Why's he coming here?" someone asked.

"Cause Dr. O wants him here. This poet's a big deal; he's got books and all."

A man—I thought poets were girls—but he's a commie dago sympathizer, I guess, too.

"Will they shock him?"

"Yeah, no doubt, you know Dr. O loves the shocker."

"Think he'll come up here?"

"Yeah, eventually, gonna do Howard's Hall—the Hole— first for a little quiet time, you know, get him straightened out."

"Yeah," the man said, looking at the aide, "This guy will have friends, a poet like that will have friends; they'll watch for him, won't they?"

"The fucking poet ain't gonna have any friends either," the aide said. "He's in for it. Fancy schoolboy bastard; he is in for it."

★ ★ ★

But in a war or in a family steeped in trauma, everyone's in for it.

The Cost of Driving Me Crazy

There is another part to the story of that day when Donald almost killed us on the highway. We did make it onto the shoulder of the road that afternoon, and I did run up and down the road screaming. And I did kick the car and I did swear at my mother, looking absolutely crazy.

But then, of course, we still had to get home.

So, on that terrible day there were only two possible drivers to get us home. My mother had never learned to drive; therefore, it would have to be Donald or me. I was scared to get behind the wheel again with Donald in the car, but I was even more afraid of him driving. This meant I would have to drive us home, and I would have to drive home the way that he wanted to go.

I got back in the car, still trembling, and I explained we would go home the way that Donald wanted, but first I would have to drive forward to find an exit to get us off the highway. I put on my flashers and proceeded to drive extremely slowly along the shoulder of the road to reach the next exit. No one spoke. We made it to the exit, turned onto the local road, and made it home in two hours.

It was dark when we got back to my mother's apartment. I didn't want any dinner, but my mother warmed up leftovers for Donald, and they sat in the living room eating and watching television.

I went into the bedroom and closed the door and dialed my brother's number. When Larry answered I said, "Donald is fucking nuts; he tried to run me off the road today."

"You let him drive?" Larry asked.

"No," I said and explained what had happened.

Larry was laughing before I finished telling him what happened. Now I was really angry. "He almost killed us; this isn't funny."

But Larry kept laughing. "I know, I know," he said, "and now you know."

After making plans to meet Larry for lunch the next day I called a friend in Baltimore, and while I talked to her about the strain of visiting my mother, I didn't mention the incident on the highway. Instead I told her of my frustration at being stuck in the small apartment with the old people. I didn't tell her about Donald, the car, or nearly dying. It was too crazy. I knew things like this, like the things that happened when I was younger, were incomprehensible to other people. But I also feared that while this incident was about my mother and Donald, craziness of this magnitude might also seem to be about me. Yes, the shame had attached to me instantly.

As I talked on the phone, I played with things on my mother's dresser. I enjoyed trying on her costume jewelry. Sometimes I'd ask her for something if I liked it. After I got off the phone, I opened her closet and looked through her clothes and shoes.

I didn't know what I was looking for. I could not have articulated it, but I wanted something. I looked at the top shelf of the closet where there were piles of shoeboxes, and I saw Donald's wallet. I didn't hesitate. I reached for it and flipped through the bill section. He had several hundred dollars. I took a one-hundred-dollar bill and shoved it in my jeans pocket. I put the wallet back up on the shelf and sat back on the bed, still staring into the closet. I stood up, took the wallet again, removed four twenties, and added them to my pocket.

I didn't know I was making a formal calculation, but I knew $100 wasn't enough; $180 was more like it.

That night I barely slept. I still had adrenaline in my bloodstream and was unnerved by seeing both Donald and my mother through new eyes. And I had the money.

The next day we met Larry for lunch at a family-style restaurant near the Pennsylvania Turnpike. Donald and I each drove our own cars, which was fine by me since I'd be driving home to Baltimore after we ate.

At lunch Larry talked about his work, and my mother talked about her neighbors, friends, and church. Donald and I sat there in silence as the two of them chatted. Larry paid for lunch. Afterward I kissed and hugged Donald and my mother good-bye and got on the road around one o'clock.

A few minutes into my drive I knew where I was going; I had seen the signs on Friday as I drove to Pittsburgh from Baltimore. Eighty miles outside Pittsburgh was the Valley Falls Outlet Shopping Center.

I turned off at the exit and quickly found the London Fog outlet. Just inside the door on a front rack was an all-season trench coat. The tag said the retail price was $250, but the markdown was good, and I took the trench coat to the counter—a size six petite, khaki color with epaulets and a zip-out wool lining for $160. Mine.

I kept that coat more than fifteen years and wore it often. Occasionally I'd remember how I came to buy it and I'd cringe, remembering that I had stolen Donald's money. Mostly it didn't cross my mind.

Now, I think about that day. Was it a penance I imposed on him? Retribution? A fine? Had the trauma, and my inability to talk about it, distorted my own values? But why that coat? Yes, I liked classic clothes, but there was more to it. I'd grown up watching *The Man from U.N.C.L.E.* and *Get Smart,* and I enjoyed detective shows of the 1970s. Spies and detectives wore trench coats.

But it's not lost on me now, years later, that a trench coat is actually a military coat. They are called trench coats because British soldiers wore them in World War I when trench warfare was commonplace. Those soldiers choked and gagged and bled and died in those long khaki coats. Was I a detective? Or was I dressing for the fight of my life?

CHAPTER SEVEN

Semper Fi: There's No Purple Heart for Falling Apart

After months of corresponding with several China Marines, I finally made plans to meet them in person. The annual China Marine Reunion was planned for October 2003 in St. Louis, Missouri. For a year we had written to each other, my new pals Frenchy, Bones, and Cliff. "God willing," we would say when we closed our letters, "God willing, I'll see you in October." And it is God willing, of course, when the team is in its eighties. Each year fewer men attend the reunion.

Frenchy tells me that he'll arrive early on Thursday to set up. He is the bartender in the hospitality suite at the hotel. I fly from Albany to Baltimore and then to St. Louis, taking a taxi to the Hilton Hotel on the edge of the city. Across the street from the Hilton Hotel is a big shopping mall with a Saks Fifth Avenue. In the hotel lobby a sign says, "Welcome China Marines."

As I unpack, I realize I am nervous. I try on a scarf, then a necklace. *Should I wear a skirt?* I am a youngster in this crowd;

these are elderly men whom I've come to feel so close to. But I have not yet told them about the murders.

I don't want them to think I will sensationalize or disrespect their experiences. I say a prayer and remind myself, *I am here to learn*. I look out my hotel window and see there is a path from the hotel to Saks Fifth Avenue. *Well, I can always shop*, I think. *If this is too weird, I'll go shopping.*

A tumble of laughter and happy voices greets me when I get off the elevator on the fifth floor. The hospitality suite is in front of me. A man at the door wearing a China Marine Reunion name tag welcomes me. I tell him I am looking for Frenchy Dupont.

"Ho ho, another gal for Frenchy," he says loudly, turning to the room. The man at the bar looks over, sets down the drink he is making, and comes over.

"Diane, I'm glad you made it," he says, opening his arms for a hug. I know this is Frenchy by his Louisiana accent and his immediate warmth.

The introductions begin. "She's writing a book about her dad; he was in, was it 1938 or 1939?" Frenchy asks me as he steers me to another group of older men.

"It was my stepfather," I explain. "He was married to my mother."

"Is he alive?"

"No," I tell them, "Donald died a couple of years ago. I'm here to learn about China and what he did there."

Frenchy takes up my case. "She needs records," he says and points to a man sitting near the window in conversation with two older men. "That's Pat Hitchcock, he knows about records. The records are here in St. Louis, but you have to write for them. Go talk to Pat." Frenchy gives me a little nudge and asks, "Want a drink? We have everything."

More people arrive, greeting each other with loud hellos. Some have canes, some have crutches, most move slowly, but I notice their posture. Most of these men stand very straight, heads high. *Marines,* I think. *They are Marines.*

Frenchy brings me the Coke I requested and says, "Meet some people. I have to work, I'm the bartender."

Later I learn that Frenchy is the bartender every year, and he always arrives a day early to set up. Someone tells me that Frenchy is legally blind. He developed beriberi in the Philippines. "I got my legs back and I beat jungle rot," he says, but his central vision never returned. He's worked for years for the Veterans Administration in Louisiana helping other veterans get their benefits and apply for health and vocational services.

The next day of the reunion, I begin with a small group near the door and introduce myself. I meet Frenchy's wife, Angela, and their daughter Teal. Teal's husband has gone sightseeing during the Marines' reunion. For the next few days, I'll stay in this room and talk to these men.

"Come over here," Bones calls to me. Again, these guys were up before me, hair brushed, shoes shined, some drinking coffee, and some already having a shot of whiskey at breakfast time.

I move in and out of conversations. These men now see how new I am to military life. They explain the structure: A regiment equals 1,000 Marines; two battalions are in a regiment; companies are subsets of regiments. Donald was part of Company G, 2nd Battalion, 6th Marines. I learn that most of the 6th Marines joined with the 4th Marines in China midway through Donald's tour. He likely went north to Tientsin with the 4th Marines after December 1937.

Each day, I have breakfast in the hotel restaurant and then go upstairs to the Marines' hospitality suite. This is the reunion: men talking, wives shopping, and grown children taking their kids to sightsee in St. Louis. I stay in the hospitality suite with the Marines, and most of the time I'm the only woman. They talk. I listen. They enjoy having a newcomer, a new audience as they reminisce. My presence brings out stories; they want to talk and they want to explain about China.

I drink Cokes, and they drink whiskey, beer, Seven and Seven—Seagram's 7 and 7Up—and straight shots of bourbon. They stop at noon to send for room service sandwiches and salad plates, and everyone takes pills with their lunch. They compare medications: heart pills, blood pressure pills, and diuretics.

The men ask about Donald and quiz me about China to see how much I know. I tread carefully talking about Donald's past. I explain that Donald had been in a hospital and had killed someone; they shake their heads. I tell them it was his first wife. They say how awful that is. No one says he is bad. Then I tell them about his mother-in-law. They shake their heads and laugh.

"I think something happened to him in China," I say.

They nod. I mention to them I have read *The Rape of Nanking* by Iris Chang. They know the book, and some saw Iris Chang interviewed. "There was a program about her on TV, wasn't there?"

Different men move in and out of the conversation each day. One day I sit with Bones who is Frenchy's friend. Bones is moving from California to Virginia in the next week to live with his daughter. This is sad news, Frenchy tells me privately, explaining that Bones is sick and can't live alone. This will probably be his last reunion. I see that Bones can hardly walk.

"He has bad legs. It's from the Philippines," Frenchy explains. They were in Palawan together, one of the infamous POW camps. "Tomorrow," he says, "tomorrow when we go to the cemetery, you'll see."

The next day is Saturday, and there are fewer people in the hospitality suite after breakfast. Today is the group's big outing to the Jefferson Barracks National Cemetery in St. Louis. Rented buses come to the hotel driveway at 11:30 a.m. Some Marines drive their own cars. I'm told that we'll see "other military" at the cemetery, and "some of it will be Army." It's said kindly, as if this is a generosity and a grace on both sides.

"We are going to dedicate a plaque, and there will be an honor guard," Frenchy says. But he is busy today and distracted.

"Frenchy's going to be one of the speakers," Bones tells me when Frenchy doesn't sit down to talk.

On the bus I sit with Frenchy's daughter, Teal. We make small talk about Plaquemine, Louisiana, where they live.

"You should come visit," she says. "My father likes talking to you." It's clear that she is not troubled that he talks so personally to a stranger.

At the cemetery Teal joins her mother and Frenchy near the podium. A small crowd has gathered a few feet off the service road that winds through the cemetery. This is a national military cemetery; all of the stones are the same creamy white marble like the headstones at Arlington National Cemetery in Washington, DC. As we wait for the service to begin, I join a small group looking at a bronze plaque that is newly installed. It's shiny, flat, and flush with the ground. Many of the Marines are bending over to photograph the plaque, which marks the burial place of the bones of 123 victims of the Palawan slaughter.

I recognize some of the people in the crowd from the hotel, but there are new faces today as well. And there are more young people today—the grandchildren. I stay in the back of the crowd, unsure of my place and unsure of the etiquette. The laughter and banter of the past two days are gone.

Another van arrives and younger soldiers step out and begin removing musical instruments; it's a military band. "The Army Reserves," someone near me whispers.

From another direction, I see another group of military men walking toward us. I feel an unexpected rush of emotion and tears as I realize that I'm looking at young Marines in parade dress—red, blue, and white uniforms with swords at their side.

The young Marines stop several yards away, and I hear the call to order. They snap to the rigid posture of attention. Frenchy walks over to the officer in charge. With serious faces, the two men salute each other and then, after a few words, Frenchy and the other man start laughing. Frenchy walks back to our group, and the other man turns on one heel and calls the honor guard to begin.

The Army musicians play "The Battle Hymn of the Republic." The honor guard presents the flags. We say the Pledge of Allegiance. A man from the crowd comes to the podium and thanks the Army Reserve musicians and the Marines from the St. Louis Reserves barracks. He explains that we are here to dedicate this plaque honoring those who died at Palawan.

My Marines look smaller and older now. They are wearing pieces of their old uniforms and an assortment of polyester caps with Marine emblems. Some wear sashes across their nylon windbreakers and golf jackets. They wear sneakers and walking shoes. Bones is wearing brown dress pants, a tan McGregor windbreaker, and bedroom slippers.

There is a prayer and more thanks. Then the man at the podium says, "Now we'll have a story."

Frenchy comes forward, and I see his eyes are red-rimmed. "There are fewer of us each year," he says, "who know what happened there." He explains there were many men killed, very few survived, and no one knows "like we do" what happened.

Frenchy introduces Glenn McDole. Glenn is wearing a bright red blazer, white shirt, black trousers, and shiny dress shoes. Pinned to the bottom of his tie is a red ribbon with gold letters that state, "Survivor of Palawan." Snow-white hair peeks out from the sides of his red polyester trucker-style cap with "Fourth Marines" in gold letters.

Glenn clears his throat several times at the podium. Then he launches into a description of Palawan and talks about the men he knew on that Philippine island. Glenn nods at people in the crowd as he mentions their names.

The Marines on Palawan were starving, sick, weak, and living like animals. They were grateful if, once a month, they could steal garbage from the Japanese kitchen. And they were tortured. Many, like Frenchy, who straightens up as his name is mentioned, went blind. They had pellagra, beriberi, blood disease, and jungle rot. Each day, naked and barefoot, they were marched into the jungle in groups of ten. Their task was to clear trees and build a landing strip for the Japanese. If one of the American prisoners tried to run away, the other nine in the unit would also be killed to dissuade others from trying to run.

Their last day was no better. In the early afternoon, they heard United States Navy planes overhead, and for a moment the Palawan prisoners hoped for rescue. But in the next minute they realized the arrival of those planes meant the Japanese would kill them.

Weeks earlier the Marines had been forced to dig a long trench, which, they were told, was an "air raid shelter." Now 141 Americans were herded at bayonet point into the ditch, tumbling on top of one another.

They listened again for the planes but then smelled gasoline. The Japanese soldiers were pouring gas from large cans onto the men in the ditch. Some men tried to push out but were not fast enough. The Japanese soldiers tossed lighted torches onto them. Roasting flesh mixed with gasoline and excrement, and 129 men burned to death.

One end of the long trench ended at a cliff, an embankment that overlooked the beach. A dozen men at that end pushed up and out of the ditch and rolled over the cliff, dropping and sliding 125 feet down the jagged rocks. The Japanese soldiers ran to the cliff edge and shot at them as they fell. Some of the Americans ran and limped along the beach with bullets in their broken legs and backs. The Japanese chased them and tortured any they caught—lighting feet and hands on fire and slicing off extremities with bayonets.

The men still able to escape were bleeding and broken. But they dove, bloody, into the sea and began to swim. Two days later, eight men came ashore on another Philippine island where civilians rescued them.

As I listen to Glenn speak, I am holding my breath. It's much worse than I had imagined. I steal some sideways looks at the crowd. The Marines stand tall; even those in wheelchairs stare straight ahead, faces grim. Family members listen, leaning and shifting their weight, and soften their posture, but they have tears running down their faces. A man near me says to his teenaged son, "Those were Grandpa's friends."

The Marines of Palawan were starved, blinded, set on fire, rolled down cliffs, and shot at while they ran; then they swam for miles, being shredded by coral and bitten by sharks. I am listening but I can't comprehend. How did those eight survive? How could they not be insane after that?

On the bus ride back to the hotel, Bones explains again about the battlefield and why it was so distressing. "There were no rules of engagement for the Japanese," he says.

"What do you mean?"

"There are rules, even in war," Bones tells me. "Most civilians don't know that, but there are. For the Japanese, though, there was no distinction between civilian and military persons, and no respect, as on other battlefields, to protect noncombatant personnel."

On several occasions Bones and the others had encountered Japanese soldiers on the battlefield who would call out "corpsman" in English, as if they were wounded and needed help. When the medic came to their aid, the Japanese soldiers would shoot him in the head.

Bones's speech is pressured. It's been an intense morning. He doesn't feel well, but he keeps turning his body toward me. He wants me to understand what happened to them in China. At first I just listen, not really sure, and then I realize he is trying to help me understand what happened to Donald.

In December 1937 the China Marines defended the International Settlement. They were there to protect American businesses and Chinese civilians. Later, when the war moved to the Philippines, soldiers in the United States Army were the first to see what happened when the American military encountered the Japanese. What they saw was unlike anything that had happened in any other war: They found American soldiers who had been butchered. Many had been buried alive or tied up and left to die in the sun. Sometimes they would find soldiers or Marines who had been disemboweled. The soldiers and the Marines found the mutilated corpses of other United States Marines who had had chunks of their flesh or their genitals cut off and stuffed into their mouths.

★ ★ ★

Saturday night is the China Marine banquet, which will be in stark contrast to this morning's ceremony.

The hospitality suite closes at four o'clock, and the men go to their rooms to shower and change. Frenchy's wife, Angela, has gone across the street to the mall to get her hair done. She wears a pretty, pale blue chiffon cocktail dress. I wish I'd brought a dress, but I wear my black pants and an embroidered shawl.

The men are wearing suits, and they have medals pinned on their jackets. Some wear their Marine caps to the dining room.

I sit between Frenchy and Angela at dinner. A man steps to the podium and calls the room to order. Silence. The clinking of glasses stops. Some younger soldiers in full dress appear at the entrance to the dining room. These are more soldiers from the St. Louis barracks who have come to present colors. An American flag and Marine Corps flag are carried in. We stand to say the Pledge of Allegiance. I peek to the side. The Marines salute. It's stern and moving. My throat is closing as I try not to cry.

Dinner is noisy and fun. The older Marines go from table to table visiting. Frenchy tells me names of men at the other tables. He hands me a pen and gestures that I should be writing this down.

When dessert is served, another man steps to the podium. He is the guest speaker and a professor of military history at nearby Washington University. He will talk about the role of the United States Marines in war. I know the men in this room know more than he does. And I realize that I, too, now know some things this historian does not.

It's now the last day; the hospitality suite is closed. We are sitting at the bar of the Hilton Hotel. I'll leave tomorrow, and Frenchy and I are having a private conversation.

"We were animals," Frenchy says. "I have one memory from China that I don't talk about much. I've never told Teal." He then shares his memory with me.

"A tangle of bodies and brush. As the fighting stops, we squint from all the dust, and I keep blinking because I don't really want to see. I'm lying on the ground, my cheek to the dirt, and I'm looking across the field. I'm slowly aware—it's a delayed reaction—that the bombs and gunfire have stopped and now I'm hearing something worse: the whimpers and moans of men in pain. I am aware of a scratching sound above my head so I carefully turn my head, keeping it low, and look around. There is a Marine ten yards away; he's on the ground, too, but he's twisted. His chest is to the dirt, but his legs are sideways; one leg is kicking, jerking powerfully. It's the heel of his boot that is digging into the dirt, making that sound. I remember wondering if it was a reflex, a death spasm, or if he was doing it on purpose. And I get nauseous.

"*Marines do not leave their dead.* It's repeating in my head like a mantra. They trained us this way. And now I know why. We can't leave them, not here, especially not here. There really is something worse than death, and China Marines know that."

Frenchy looks at me, and I look at him. I'm not following.

He continues. "Weeks before, we had come upon another field after a battle, and our dead were all over the ground. My men began to go to them, to see who was alive or injured, and I heard men gagging and retching. I looked down at the bodies near me and, yes, they were dead, but worse than that. They'd been all cut up. The men on the ground were cut open and soaked in blood. They were cut apart, ears cut off, hands cut off; it was like meat, that's all there is, it was like meat. . . . I can't describe it. These were men we ate with, rode with, and played ball with.

"They were . . ." He pauses. "Okay, I'll tell you. They were cut at the waist . . . their male parts, their genitals, had been cut off, and they were left on the ground, or, how can I say this? Their male parts were in the dead men's mouths. Who would tell a wife or a sweetheart or a mother about that? To know he died in battle, fighting, crawling, and screaming, isn't that enough?"

I can think of nothing to say. He looks at me, and then he continues.

"I remember once, later, after we had seen that field and all those men cut like that . . . we looked for all the hands and tried to bury them. Well, later, after that, we must have been in the Philippines by then, it was another battle, and the Japanese were close by. We were there, and the medics began to come, coming to help us. We were getting up as the medics arrived, and there was this guy near me, and one of the medics was starting to help a Marine near him, and as the medic opened his knife to cut the shirt off the injured man, this guy near me jumps up, screaming like blood, and he starts to attack the medic. This Marine is attacking the medic—our medic—and he's twisting his neck. We had to pull him off the medic and knock him out. He was going to kill the medic like he was a Jap."

I tell Frenchy how grateful I am to learn all of this—even the awful things—and I tell him that I am sad and trying to comprehend what I've heard. The horror is so much worse than I expected. How did they survive in China? And how did they survive after coming home?

"Does some of this explain Donald?" he asks me.

I nod. "But the racism; it's racism, isn't it?" I ask him. I've heard the ugly words all week.

"Racism or hatred?" he asks me. "Is there a difference between racism and hating the enemy, between racism and knowing some things?"

I can't speak.

"Diane," Frenchy says, "I would never let my grandchildren say the words I do, but I hate them, all of them. I have to."

Donald at the Barracks in Tientsin—1939

Each time he bent to pick up his clothes or a towel, even when he played ball with Dante, he'd get that rush of sick feeling. He'd tried to shake it off; he even stopped drinking for a week, but it was still there. It wasn't from the food; the chow was good. The mess in Tientsin had a great, enlisted Army cook, and they had a Chinese cook, too, so they got great food. They couldn't go to restaurants up here in Tientsin like in Shanghai; they couldn't get the French and German food like they had there, but this was good.

He sat on his bunk and lowered his head into his hands for a minute. His head hurt. He tried to think about when it had started. He'd taken that whack from a rifle butt a month ago. They'd been drilling, and when part of the unit stepped out, he was too close and took the butt on the back of his head. The noise was the loudest part. He'd ended up in sick bay for two days; they had to watch in case he had a concussion, but nothing came of that. He remembered seeing stars, though, and how he'd realized why they say that; he really saw flickering lights just like stars when he went down.

No, maybe he needed to sleep more, or maybe it was some nutrition problem. Pearl, who had been a fellow foster child when Donald was young, had sent him clippings from the Pittsburgh paper about how you were supposed to take iron tablets for your blood. She was always after him to take vitamin remedies and eat liver. He hated that.

He rose and walked toward the end of the barracks to the head. "It'll pass," he told himself; he wasn't going back to the sick bay for a headache. There'd be no end of the teasing that'd come from that. "Got your monthly, Watkins? Need some aspirin and a Kotex?"

This was not so bad, being up here. The guys were okay, though there were a couple he'd rather avoid, those who did the pushing and bullying. Some of the stuff they said got him mad. Dante would always say to him, "Hey, that's just Marine talk; it's the same as in basic. Don't listen to them."

It wasn't like basic, though, he thought. In basic the drill sergeant could call a man any name: faggot, queer, and sissy girl. They would call a guy a "sissy girl" to try to get him mad, to see if he'd take a swing. If he dared, they'd kick his ass. But that was all about testing a man to see what he was made of; he knew that.

But up in Tientsin, it was some of the men in his bunk who called him those names. They were guys who'd recently joined them and had come up from Peiping; they didn't know him from the 6th. These guys were always trying to make something of the fact that he'd been to college.

"Hey, college boy," they'd say. "Got one of those plaid skirts, Donnie?"

"Ignore them, Watkins," Dante would say when he'd see him marching out of the barracks, steaming. "You have the marks, you have the ratings, and they don't."

The tension in the barracks had gotten worse lately because he'd gone off on someone last week. He had pushed a guy and told him, "Shut your fucking mouth." Everyone else had laughed the guy off, but he'd spun around and blew up at the guy. Dante jumped between them and then dragged him out to play ball. But he knew he left himself open, and he regretted that.

But now his stomach wasn't right, his head hurt if he lowered it at all, and he had no patience for crap from those guys. Why were they calling him names? He'd gone to the whores like the rest, and he'd had a couple of girls in Shanghai. They knew what they were doing, and he got his money's worth.

He came back to the barracks again and started to dress to sit out on the steps and read his magazine. *Fresh air,* he thought, *fresh air would make me feel better.*

He heard the other guys coming back; their shouts were clear as they came into the compound.

"We got some Coca-Cola," they called out.

A guy from farther down yelled, "Hey, save me a Coke, I'll be over."

4th Marine Regiment Color Guard, circa 1937

US Marines recruiting posters Donald would have seen growing up

Donald and the other men from the 6th Marine Regiment
arrive in Shanghai on the USS *Chaumont*, September 19, 1937.

6th Marine Regiment aboard the
USS *Chaumont*, September 19, 1937

Nanking Road was the principal retail business street in
Shanghai, China. Marines could have purchased almost any
foreign goods in the first three blocks of the street.

The Bund was often the first stop for visitors in Shanghai.
The west side included modern buildings, and the east side
was the edge of the Whangpoo River.

A business card for the Venus Café in Shanghai, which was one of
the most lively places in town for Marines to visit

On December 13, 1937, Senator Robert Reynolds (right)
spoke to the Senate about the sinking of the USS *Panay*
and declared that the United States might regret its failure
to withdraw gunboats and Marines from Chinese waters.
Senator David I. Walsh (left), Chairman of the Senate Foreign
Relations Committee, is pictured with Reynolds.

Senators Gerald P. Nye and Henry Cabot Lodge (right)
were part of the group of senators insisting that President
Roosevelt invoke the Neutrality Act to keep the United
States out of the Sino-Japanese conflict, 1937.

Soochow Creek separated Shanghai and Hongkew.

Chinese soldiers set fire to Hongkew so the Japanese could
take over only burnt buildings.

(top) Sandbags stacked to protect Marines on Soochow Creek
(bottom) Marines standing guard on Shanghai side
of Soochow Creek

(top) Heavily shelled building in Hongkew
(bottom) Bombed out building in Hongkew

273   **Nanking Under Japanese Rule**

The population of Nanking before the Japanese invasion was about 1,000,000, but today it is only about 250,000 composed of the poorest class Chinese, students, intellectuals, and officials. Japanese Army and Navy men are plentiful. The great Chungshan highway that runs through Nanking is alive with speeding Japanese army trucks bearing soldiers and supplies to various points. The drivers are very reckless, and pedestrians are in danger of their lives when they venture out in the road, as the picture shows. Although there is sufficient food, other conveniences are few. There is no telephone service, streets are unlighted, and the water supply is turned off every evening. There appears to be no garbage or sewage disposal, and the dead are left where they fall. Nobody, not even a foreigner, may enter or leave the city through the gates of the wall unless accompanied by a Jap policeman.

To know the HORRORS OF WAR is to want PEACE

This is one of the SECOND SERIES of Horrors of War picture cards and true stories of today's warfare. Save to get a complete history. Copyright 1938, Gum, Inc., Phila., Pa. Printed in U.S.A.

The 1938 Gum Inc. Horrors of War cards depicted the Spanish Civil War, the Ethiopian War, and the Chinese-Japanese War.

The main building at St. Elizabeths Hospital,
Washington, DC, circa 1930

Farview State Hospital, Waymart, Pennsylvania, circa 1940

Murder Charged In Killings

"Jealousy" Held As Motive For Slaying Wife, Mother-In-Law

Watkins Views Body Of His Bride

Watkins In Hospital After Marine Service; Good Worker, Capable

Donald Watkins Goes To Farview

Double Slayer Is Adjudged Insane

Headlines from *Washington Observer* articles, 1953

National Cemetery, St. Louis, Missouri (left to right) Glenn McDole, Frenchy Dupont, Bobby Bacon, Frank Galligan, John Boswell, George Burleigh, and Lou Curtis

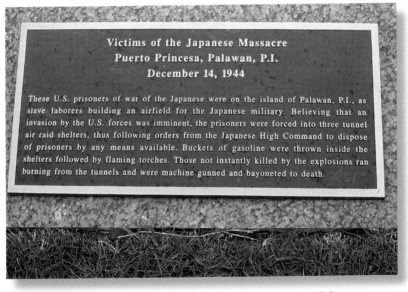

Victims of the Japanese Massacre
Puerto Princesa, Palawan, P.I.
December 14, 1944

These U.S. prisoners of war of the Japanese were on the island of Palawan, P.I., as slave laborers building an airfield for the Japanese military. Believing that an invasion by the U.S. forces was imminent, the prisoners were forced into three tunnel air raid shelters, thus following orders from the Japanese High Command to dispose of prisoners by any means available. Buckets of gasoline were thrown inside the shelters followed by flaming torches. Those not instantly killed by the explosions ran burning from the tunnels and were machine gunned and bayoneted to death.

Memorial honoring the victims of the Japanese massacre at Palawan

Glenn and Frenchy

4th Marine reunion in 2001 (left to right) Angela Dupont,
Frenchy, John Craig, and Diane

Cliff and Sylvia Wells, 1988

Diane and her mother, Florence, 1989

Florence with Donald at her seventy-fifth birthday party

So, he thought, *they're going to be in here drinking and shooting the breeze all afternoon; that'd mean the big mouth would be starting in on me again.* He pulled his shirt back off and reached for his T-shirt and shorts.

"Hey, Caruso," he called out the window, "let's go play; let's have a game, okay?"

★ ★ ★

I have to file several Freedom of Information Act requests to get Donald's military records from the National Personnel Records Center. They show the course of Donald's experience in the spring of 1939.

On March 1, 1939, there was a disturbing incident in the Tientsin barracks. The officer in charge wrote in that day's log that "Donald Watkins on returning to the barracks and, in an insane fit, attacked his friend Dante Caruso and another Marine." On that day Donald was admitted to the sick bay. He remained there in a "quiet room" guarded by two sentries. Due to his "maniacal behavior," he was moved to a "confinement cell" where, the medical survey noted, "restraining apparatus has been necessary on several occasions."

On April 21, 1939, Donald was taken to the German-American Hospital in Tientsin, a civilian hospital, for a head x-ray. The medical record of the German-American Hospital states that two months prior to the incident in the barracks, "the patient received a head injury. An x-ray deemed advisable to eliminate any bone pathology."

Then, on May 18, 1939, Donald was again aboard the USS *Chaumont* departing from the port of Chinwangtao and sailing for San Francisco. On July 6, he was admitted to the Ware Island United States Naval Hospital where Donald's admissions record states his diagnosis is "dementia praecox," and the "patient was received in a draft of insane mental cases" from the West Coast.

The next day Donald was transferred to St. Elizabeths Hospital in Washington, DC.

I keep reading about war. The history books are helpful, but not enough. Like the man who spoke at the St. Louis reunion, I know now that my Marines know things that no one wrote about. I look to memoir and even poetry.

I think about the sex and the food and the music in Shanghai. I think about those young men, so full of life and libido, spending their days with death. And I think about Donald.

★ ★ ★

For my mother's seventy-fifth birthday, we plan a surprise party in Pittsburgh. Her five children, grandchildren, and some old friends meet at a restaurant on the north side. My sister Joy has come from California, and that is the real surprise for my mother. Joy was the first to move away and the one who rarely comes home.

Larry has invited my mother and Donald out to dinner, and when he brings them into the restaurant we all shout, "Surprise!" My mother is thrilled. Donald looks confused, but he settles in to listen to stories, piecing together who is who in his bride's life. He has his arm around the back of my mother's chair and is gracious with her friends. It is a memorable night for the surprise and for the easy happiness, and because, while we did not know it then, it would be the last time that we would all be together.

Four weeks later my brother-in-law calls from California to say that Joy has died. She had been very ill for months and had not told us.

My mother is undone by Joy's death, and her grief becomes mania. When we meet at the airport to fly to Los Angeles, my mother is buying greeting cards in the gift shop.

"Look at these adorable cards. I'm buying all my birthday cards for the coming year."

I'm furious that she does not seem sad. I look at Donald, who is holding my mother's handbag, and as he pats my back he says, "I am so sorry about your sister, so very sorry for your loss."

CHAPTER EIGHT

They Brought Home More Than Souvenirs

World War I was the United States' first full-scale entry into armed conflict on European soil. War has changed since then, and we have changed, but there is one constant—the sad fact of psychological injuries sustained by soldiers in war.

Various authorities—military and psychiatric—estimate that "stress casualties" affect 30 to 70 percent of all soldiers. Our attitude toward mental breakdown in soldiers has shifted with each war, and the words we use for it have changed over time. Some of the terms we've used for psychiatric casualties include shell shock, trench suicide, battle fatigue, soldier's heart, war neurosis, military hysteria, and Post-Vietnam Syndrome.

In World War I when military manpower and recruiting strength were good, soldiers who broke down, froze on the field, or hesitated to shoot could be court-martialed or diagnosed as having LMF—Lacking Moral Fiber.

Later, in the 1940s, as demographics changed and the United States had fewer men at the time we were engaged in battle in both Asia and Europe, it became crucial to retain every possible fighting man. We had to reframe what was then called "shell shock." In order to return soldiers to the front as quickly as possible and to decrease the growing disability debt that the United States government was facing, the Pentagon began to invest in research on psychological injury and the treatment of mental disorders.

War trauma then became an "illness" that could be "treated."

More than any other war, Vietnam redefined our perceptions about mental illness. Five years after the fall of Saigon, "Post-Vietnam Syndrome" was identified, which later morphed into "post-traumatic stress disorder," which was then generalized to include civilians who suffer other kinds of trauma.

Post-traumatic stress disorder didn't exist during the Vietnam War. In 1960 the diagnostic term "gross stress reaction" had been removed from the *DSM, The Diagnostic and Statistical Manual of Mental Disorders*—the bible of psychiatry. But in 1970, a group of Vietnam veterans in New York City began to meet informally in "rap groups" to talk about their frightening and troublesome symptoms that we now recognize as PTSD.

A May 6, 1972, article in *The New York Times* by Chaim "Hy" Shatan used the term "Post-Vietnam Syndrome" to describe what was happening to some Vietnam veterans and how their symptoms—anger, fear, paranoia, rage, nightmares, flashbacks, and sudden outbursts of violent behavior—were paralyzing their lives and destroying their families.

According to Shatan, Post-Vietnam Syndrome would typically set in nine to thirty months after a soldier's return from Asia. Men would notice, often for the first time, apathy, cynicism, and paranoia, as well as restlessness, nightmares, and a propensity toward violence or suicide. They were suffering, Shatan said, "from delayed massive trauma, guilt, self-punishment, and alienation from their feelings."

Many of those veterans, who sought help like others before them, had been misdiagnosed as schizophrenics and had been subjected to additional torments with treatments that ranged from debilitating antipsychotic medications to electroconvulsive therapy, or "shock treatment." The veterans, through their constant challenges at regional VA hospitals, appealed to the Pentagon for help.

The strategy proposed by Shatan was to get the diagnosis "Post-Vietnam Syndrome" into the *DSM*, which would allow veterans to be classified as disabled and get their psychiatric treatment paid for by the Veterans Administration. But, according to Shatan, there was fear that the United States Treasury couldn't fund the treatment.

The turning point came in 1975 when a small group of Vietnam veterans held the head of the United States Department of Veterans Affairs as a hostage in his Washington, DC, office, forcing him to review the data they had collected and hear the impact of this Post-Vietnam Syndrome. They described how more and more Vietnam veterans were committing suicide, being convicted of crimes, being lost to addiction and homelessness, and being committed to long stays in mental hospitals.

Over the next ten years, as research on Post-Vietnam Syndrome expanded, medical and psychiatric personnel documented similar symptoms in survivors of traumatic events like earthquakes and rape. By 1980, post-traumatic stress disorder became a standardized definition in the *DSM-III*. And today, after Major Depression, PTSD is the most widely used diagnosis in the *DSM-5*.

In 1946, when Donald returned to Washington, Pennsylvania, from his stay at St. Elizabeths Hospital, he was welcomed as a veteran returning from war. He was thirty-five years old. Other veterans were returning at the same time from Europe, the Pacific, and hospitals, so it would not have seemed unusual. And Donald was, in fact, an honorably discharged Marine who had defended his country.

In that town, as in all towns across America, citizens were prepared to welcome home their soldiers and help them make new lives. Despite fears that the postwar economy would not be able to reabsorb the returning soldiers, postwar consumerism created a boom that led to plenty of jobs. In the industrial center of Western Pennsylvania, where the production of coal, steel, aluminum, and glass was abundant, the job market was good for veterans.

There was also a barrage of information on the home front to help families reorient their veterans to domestic life. The psychological problems of the returning veterans were discussed in novels, plays, radio shows, and women's magazines. Wives and girlfriends were exhorted by "experts" to rebuild their man's ego by giving him "lavish and undemanding affection" and "expecting no immediate return." Wives were advised to be forgiving of wartime infidelities and to surrender their "newly found economic independence." And for the girls who had waited out a lonely period during the war, there was an extra urgency to rush headlong into marriage when the men came home.

The Lunacy Commission

In May of 1953, two months after killing his mother-in-law and his wife, Donald was examined by a Lunacy Commission at the Washington County Jail and was declared "legally and medically insane." The Lunacy Commission consisted of a local attorney, Austin Murphy, Esq., and two local physicians, Paul

Proudfoot, MD, and Bernard Berman, MD. Both doctors were general practitioners from the town.

The report of the Lunacy Commission states, "They met in an office at the County Jail on the 7th day of May, 1953, AD, and then and there examined the said Donald K. Watkins" and "heard the statements of said prisoner and conversed with him generally." They also reported that they examined photocopies of Donald's medical history taken from Veterans Administration files. Their conclusion: "Donald K. Watkins is in fact insane and is in such a condition as to make necessary that he be cared for in a hospital for mental diseases."

The next day, May 8, 1953, the Lunacy Commission report was given to Judge Cummins who, that same day, ordered Donald committed to Farview State Hospital in Eastern Pennsylvania, near Scranton.

CHAPTER NINE

When My Mother Told Me

It was late August of 1985. My mother and Donald had been married for a little over a month, but he'd been in my mother's life for over a year. I drove to Pittsburgh for that Labor Day weekend. I wanted to see my brother Larry to talk to him about my work, and it was easiest to stay at my mother's—she had an extra bedroom.

When I arrived at my mother's, I hung my clothes in the extra bedroom and asked my mother what time Larry would be coming over.

"I want to have lunch with you today," she told me. I was a little surprised because my mother liked to have all of her kids together whenever she had the chance. So I was curious, but I said okay.

Later I wondered if Donald knew what she was going to tell me. Had she said to him at breakfast, "Don, when Diane gets here, I'd like to speak to her about your past"? But I don't think they were that organized. I imagine it was more like my mother turning to Donald when she heard me buzz up from the lobby and saying, "I'm going to take Diane out to lunch and tell her." But by then I was at the door, all smiles and suitcases, with a gift bag of candy, flowers, and magazines.

As I was unpacking, the phone rang, and my mother answered. I could tell it was Larry calling. "She just got here," my mother said. "Uh-huh, no, we're going out to lunch. . . . No, we're going out to lunch now," she said into the phone.

"Okay, okay, but wait," I heard my mother say to Larry. "Just let me do it myself," she said, cutting him off. Then she handed the phone to me and walked away. "Larry wants to talk to you."

"Hi, Lar, I just got here, and we're going out to lunch. . . . Yeah, just me and Mum." I allowed my inflection to rise, hoping he might give me a clue about this change in our schedule.

"Yeah, yeah," he boomed, "call me after you talk to Mum, okay?" There was a funny tone in his voice.

"Why?" I asked, looking toward my mother who was pretending not to eavesdrop. I wanted to know what I was walking into. If my mother wanted to talk to me without Donald and without Larry, then I suspected that my older brother Sigmund was in trouble again. Sig had been in trouble over the years. He'd lost jobs and been gambling. Last year he'd left his second wife and two young children. My mother paid the bills he'd left behind.

So what has Sig done now? I wondered. Something she didn't want Donald to know? But maybe it was something about her. Was she ill? She did have arthritis. Also, a few years earlier she'd had a small stroke, and I knew her knees gave her terrible pain. We didn't have cancer in our family; my father had a fatal stroke many years ago. But if this were a health problem, wouldn't Larry have told me?

"Just call me after lunch," Larry said. I agreed and hung up the phone.

We put on our coats and walked down the hall to the elevator. My mother walked slowly, grimacing at the pain in her knee. She was carrying several bags as usual: a bag of trash, "since we're going downstairs," and a bag of coupons to leave on the "sharing table" in the lobby. It was a senior citizen apartment building, so there were handrails everywhere and cute posters and flyers announcing bingo and blood pressure screenings. Each door along the hallway had a decorative wreath with silk flowers and a cute welcome mat, even though the hallway was carpeted. Senior citizen décor. It made me cringe.

The elevator stopped several times as we descended to the lobby, and each time, as someone got on, my mother would say, "This is my youngest; she's from Baltimore." The other person was never named. Nor was I. Just my place in the family lineup. It seemed like a senior citizen protocol, which perhaps accommodated the collective memory problems or conceded that the visitors had no real interest in knowing to whom they were being introduced.

Maybe it was a way to show off having children, children who came to visit. That was a kind of senior status symbol. They all had kids and grandkids, so that game was over, but ones who actually came to visit and from far away, that was a measure of status; hence "my youngest from Baltimore."

When we got to the mall, I dropped my mother at the entrance and went to park my car. I was only three hours in Pittsburgh and I was already, as usual, calculating how many more hours until I could leave. Part of it was my impatience with the slow pace necessitated by my mother's knees and the tedium of the many steps to do simple things, such as leave an apartment building and drive up the road to have lunch.

But it was also because in that short time I'd slammed— again—into my unrealistic expectations about what this visit could be. I wanted to be a good daughter to a good mother; I wanted us to have a nice relationship; I wanted to talk about real things. We did talk now more than we ever had in the past. She knew about my life—the therapy and the twelve-step recovery—but she didn't really keep track. She knew I worked in a school, but she didn't remember what I did. She knew I had a boyfriend but didn't remember his name. Each time I came home to visit, it became clear again that we were as close as we were going to be. I could taste my own disappointment.

But she'd asked me to lunch today, and I could feel myself hoping that maybe this was a moment. Clearly something was up. *And no,* I thought as I walked from the parking garage, *it couldn't be a health problem; she was too chipper for that.* When I met her at the mall door, she was perched on a bench like she was the mall's official welcome person and was talking to people, commenting on cute kids and telling older folks about her knees. "Bad knees," she'd say. "My daughter had to park the car."

I felt parental. There were other women my age with strollers and toddlers, but I had my mother. We went to the food court, and I installed her at a table where she immediately struck up a conversation with an older couple at the next table. Again I heard, "This is my youngest; she's from Baltimore." I went to get the food.

As we began to eat, my mother began to pull coupons and flyers from her handbag, narrating the pile of paper she put on the table. "We should go to Kaufmann's, they have nice sweaters. Do you want a sweater? And Clinique has a giveaway—do you still like Clinique?" She would randomly include the couple at the next table in her conversation; "She lives in Baltimore, they have that nice Inner Harbor there. It's nice, but they don't have a Kaufmann's." We finished our food as the older couple got up to leave. My mother started to gather her belongings.

"What did you want to tell me about Sig?" I touched her arm to stop her.

"About Sig?"

"Yeah, you wanted us to have lunch alone so you could talk to me about Sig, right?"

"No, not Sig." She seemed irritated now and put her handbag back on the seat beside her. "Not Sig, not Sig. But I do want to tell you about something." She began to resettle into her chair.

Now she was rummaging around in her plastic tote bag for something; it looked like a letter. She handed it across the table to me; it was thick with many pages of handwritten lined paper and had been refolded many times. "Donald gave this to me, and I carry it in my bag. You can have it; it's about psychology, and you can read it later."

"What is it?"

"He wrote it in the hospital."

"When was Donald in the hospital?" Now I am thinking that maybe Donald had a health problem that my mother wanted to talk about. Maybe he'd been to the doctor and heard some bad news.

"When was Donald in the hospital?" I repeat, and again my mother's face changed. This was a different look, not mad, maybe sad. She started to watch people walking by. I ran through my mental checklist of feelings, and then it hit me: she looked scared.

"Is something wrong with Donald?" I asked her, thinking it would be sad if now, so newly married, he were seriously ill.

She stared at me through a long breath, and then she suddenly burst into laughter as she covered her mouth. She was nodding her head and laughing. This made no sense. If something was wrong with him, why was she laughing?

"What is it? What is wrong with him?" I was leaning across the table, worried and confused.

She leaned in, too, and looked to the side where the couple had been, but no one was there now.

"He used to be crazy," she said.

"Crazy?" I asked "Like Mayview crazy?" Mayview was the state mental hospital near Pittsburgh; it was "the looney bin" kids joked about. When I was in grade school, a neighbor had been sent to Mayview after she had a baby, and the women in the neighborhood gossiped about that for years. I'd also worked with some patients from Mayview years ago when I did a dance therapy internship.

My mother just looked at me. I was going to have to help her tell me what was going on. I remembered Larry saying, "Call me after you talk to Mum."

"Do Sig and Larry know?" I asked, already knowing the answer.

"Yes," she said.

"Did Donald used to be in Mayview?"

"Well, a hospital like that," she said. Now it felt like we were playing the Twenty Questions guessing game.

"Was it recently or a long time ago?"

"He was there for twenty-two years."

I just stared. Puzzle pieces were rearranging themselves in my head: Donald's weirdness, his silence, and his farm that Larry called "the shack." My mother looked really nervous now, and nervous was not something my mother ever showed. She was extraverted and provocative. There had to be more. I remember thinking, *Maybe he killed someone,* but then I thought, *No, you go to jail for that, not to a hospital.*

My mother kept staring. And I stared back. People near us got up from their table, and new people sat down. I was peripherally aware of the music on the mall soundtrack and the bustle of people going by, but my mother and I sat looking at each other. She wanted me to figure it out. She wanted me to say it.

"Which hospital was he in?"

"Farview," she said. "It's near Scranton, on the other side of the state."

This was not good news; I could feel the Rolodex in my head flipping little pages. What did I know about hospitals near Scranton? I had lived in State College and in Williamsport. I knew about Allenwood Prison; it was the "country club" prison where the Watergate guys had been. But I knew there was a hospital for the criminally insane near Scranton. Those words rose to the surface: *criminally insane*. Were we really having this conversation?

There was another long pause.

"A hospital for the criminally insane?"

My mother looked at me evenly. She was not going to give. But I would win this round of the guessing game. I spoke again, looking at her straight in the eyes.

"Who did he kill?"

"His wife," she said as she stared back at me.

Wham! I felt the simultaneous rush of being right—what a smart girl am I—and an equally strong rush of cold fear. I didn't want to be right about this. I wanted my mother to be angry now; I wanted her to say, "Kill? You think he killed someone? What a terrible thing to think of Donald." But she didn't say that.

Wife? I had a vague idea that I had known Donald was married before. I must have asked my mother last year if Donald had been married or if he had kids. I'd assumed he was a widower; my mother was a widow, and he was marrying her, so maybe he was widowed, too.

Then I had a weird realization: Donald *was* a widower; even if he killed his wife, he'd still be a widower. That was a strange fact. Had none of us asked what Donald's wife died from? My mother was a widow because my father had a stroke; we went to the ICU, we waited three days, and then my father died.

What should I ask next? Do I know anyone who killed a spouse? In my high school there was that girl whose father killed her mother and then shot himself.

"You better tell me," I said to my mother. "Tell me what Larry knows."

She sighed. "Well," she began, "Donald had a nervous breakdown. He was young; he lived with his mother-in-law and had a nervous breakdown. He was very unhappy living with his mother-in-law; they didn't have a house of their own, and his mother-in-law wasn't very nice to him."

Why is she talking about his mother-in-law if it was the wife who died? Who kills their wife because they don't like their mother-in-law?

My mother was staring at me again. *Oh no, is there more to this story?* She just told me that Donald had a nervous breakdown and how much he hated his mother-in-law. But his wife was dead.

Silence. More staring.

I finally I said out loud, "Donald killed his wife *and* his mother-in-law?"

My mother didn't say anything. She was looking around again. *Has anyone heard what I just said?*

She looked back at me and said, "It was a long time ago; it wasn't like now. He grew up very poor, and he had a very hard life."

I knew she thought she was explaining something, but what I really knew in that moment was that she had *not* denied what I had just said: Donald had killed his wife and his mother-in-law.

We did not finish the conversation at that table. Both of us had had more than we could take. I couldn't form the questions I wanted to ask—when and why—but especially the one that scared me most. How had he killed them? I was too afraid to ask how.

But I also knew I had to ask those questions in the next hour. I knew I could not ask any more questions after we got back to the apartment. Now I knew why we were having lunch alone. "And Larry knows all this?"

She nodded. We got up; gathered our bags, trays, and napkins; found the trash containers; and then headed to the ladies' room. I held my mother's bags and leaned against the wall of the food court outside the washroom. When she came out I helped her put on her coat, and while her back was to me, I asked, "Did he kill them at the same time?"

Her back stiffened slightly. "Yes," she said without turning, "he had a breakdown. It was very sad."

I knew that that was the important truth of our conversation. I knew that whatever details I might later learn from my brothers—and they would be bad—Donald's story was sad. I had begun to like this older man and knew he loved my mother. Donald was old and odd, and he loved my mother, an equally odd, older woman, and so whatever had happened years before was surely very sad. But I was trying hard to push away my thoughts of two dead women.

CHAPTER TEN

Cold Storage: Farview State Hospital

"What do you know about body handlers?" Bessel van der Kolk asks me. He is one of the world's experts on trauma, and we are having lunch in a small cafe at Kripalu, a yoga retreat center in western Massachusetts. This weekend van der Kolk is leading a workshop called "Trauma and the Body." Kripalu is not the kind of place where you expect a conversation about mutilation, slaughter, and sexual torture. But when van der Kolk asks me about body handlers, I immediately remember Cliff Wells, a China Marine, who ten years earlier had said to me, "So Diane, do you know what hand-to-hand combat means?"

And again I have that disheartening feeling that while I thought I knew something, I'm about to find out that I really don't. So I say to van der Kolk, "Body handlers?"

"Google it," he tells me.

So at van der Kolk's suggestion I search for "body handlers," and it turns out there is an entire field of trauma research dedicated to the traumatic effects on those who handle dead or mutilated bodies. In the body-handling field, there are even specialized categories related to natural disasters, accidents, mass murders, terrorism, and war.

Oh God, I think, *the stuff we don't know and don't want to know.* But van der Kolk, still eating his lunch, begins to describe some of the scenarios.

When people jumped out of the World Trade Center towers in 2001, we may have said to ourselves, *Oh, they probably just disintegrated on landing.* No. The so-called "rubble" at the World Trade Center was not only concrete and stone. Yes, we heard about the DNA tests and imagined it was all small particulate matter; while some of it was like that, a lot of it was arms, legs, bones, and skin that had to be handled. Or after Hurricane Katrina—all the bodies in the flooded houses—maybe we imagined they dissolved in water like Alka-Seltzer tablets. No.

Still chewing, van der Kolk nods at me. "People don't want to hear this, don't want to think about it. We leave this work to others; we always have."

I think about China and our young Marines, like Donald, whose daily task was picking up bodies, arms and legs, or the tiny fetuses on the ground near their recent wombs.

"I worked with Holocaust survivors," van der Kolk says, "and the experts who know both—experts on the Holocaust and the Japanese from those years—all say the Japanese were much more sadistic than the Nazis."

I think again of Iris Chang, my conversation with her, the many interviews she did, and this sentence from her book, *The Rape of Nanking:* "The dogs in Nanking were so bloated from eating human flesh all day every day that they waddled."

Donald Inside Farview—1954

He froze. There was a body near his feet. The body was naked, not moving. His brain wasn't really working. His surprise, he realized, was that he felt the jolt in his chest. It took a whole second to realize he had startled. What was this? Surprise? Fear? How long since he had felt anything? Days, maybe longer? He couldn't remember. His head was filled with fog and sand, but he was awake, standing up and awake.

His head hurt badly. He kept looking at the body. He knew bodies and had seen bodies, dead bodies. He shivered and stepped back. He looked closer. This one wasn't dead. It was a man; a man all beaten up from a fight? Battle? The body had bruises; blood was near the face and blood ran from the nose.

He looked up. He was in a hallway, green walls, gray floor, and a toilet a few feet away. He felt pressure in his groin. He was on the way to the toilet—that was it. He looked at the man on the floor and stepped past him carefully. He could feel warmth in his skin now, his own blood in him, and he could hear again, as the feeling returned to his feet and fingers; something was waking up inside him, something leaving him. His head hurt, though; it pulled at him, made his hair hurt. *What is this like? It's something I know.* Then he remembered, *A hangover, I'm hung over, but it's a bad one, not like any whiskey drunk. What did I drink?*

He was sitting on the toilet now. His bowels gurgled. *Did I drink?* he wondered. Looking again at the feet of the man a few yards away, he remembered, *I didn't drink; I'm in this place, but I'm hung over. Pills, they gave me pills; pills make me drunk, make me sleep, and make me lost.*

Out. Must get out. How do I get out? Where are the other Marines? No; no Marines here. Japs? No, the pills came from guards, not Marines. Hospital. Prison. Then a sick feeling: He remembered another body on a floor, pretty legs, a woman's legs—dead. He leaned over and began to retch. He could see her legs on the floor; she was dead. He was retching and shitting at the same time. *I want to be drunk again,* he thought. *Be drunk now; make this stop.*

But raising his head to wipe his mouth, he saw the man on the floor move; he heard a groan. *That one's alive; they beat him, Jap guards beat him. No,* he reminded himself, *not Japs, the brig. I'm in the brig.* He looked at the walls. *No, not the brig, a jail, they brought me to a prison, came in a car, long drive.* But when? How long was it? A week? A month?

He closed his eyes. He was trapped, trapped again. He could hear a voice, remembered a voice, and squeezed his eyes tighter. "You are a United States Marine. You are a member of the finest corps of men in the world. Marines kill what they eat and eat what they kill. Marines do not leave their dead."

He sat straighter, stiffened. His back hurt. He grabbed the rough paper and wiped his ass, slowly stood, and pulled the thin cotton pants around his waist again.

Man down, he thought and started to call out "medic" but stopped himself. *Enemy nearby. Quiet.* He had to hide, escape, and survive. He remembered the stories he had heard at Tientsin. He remembered sitting in the barracks, the men who talked at night, Dante and George, the handball games, laughing, and the stories from the men who'd been in the Jap jail. They said, "Remember, you're a fucking Marine; you do what you have to do; you watch everything; you remember everything; you get out; and you tell somebody—you get yourself out."

He leaned against the wall, thoughts slowly forming: *No pills, the pills trap me; torture is better. Stay conscious; watch them. Learn how this works. Watch what happens.* His heart pounded, fear surged through him, and he wanted to retch again, shit again, but there was nothing. *The pills would stop this; pills will make me numb, make it all stop, make me sleep again. I need a pill or a drink or something.*

"Suck it up." He heard a voice from boot camp—no, not boot camp; it was Bemis in Shanghai. "Stand the fuck up, Watkins, you fuck. Get your fucking head out of your fucking ass and get to your fucking bunk, you pussy whiner."

He stepped away from the wall and stood straight, and his arms dropped to his sides. He walked around the body near his feet that was still, slowly now, trying to move.

He needed a map and a plan. He could come back for this guy when he got a map. He shook his head. He was in a fucking psycho ward prison; there was no map. His chest fell. *Fuck. But a plan; there's always a plan; you can make a fucking plan.* He looked down the hall again. He had come from a room down there. *Find that room again, see who else is here, what they know. What's the chain of command? Prisoner?* Maybe he was, but he was a Marine.

He walked back to the toilet again and took some of the folded paper from the shelf. He walked to the man on the floor and laid the papers near the man's bloody face, slowly pushing the papers to the man's nose. *There, soldier,* he thought, *that will hold you for now.*

★ ★ ★

The story in the *Washington Observer* on Saturday, May 9, 1953, includes reactions by the district attorney, Ray G. Zelt, who remarked:

> Most dismaying to me is the fact that this man was classified by federal authorities as suffering from dementia praecox of a paranoid type and that under these circumstances the man should be released on an innocent public to commit a heinous crime.

When I read those words, I felt Donald's story echoing across time.

But more tragic is the comment by George Stegenga, Donald's own attorney. When told that the Lunacy Commission had found Donald to be insane, Stegenga told reporters:

It merely confirms the suspicions that I have had since I was retained in the case shortly after the shooting occurred. . . . I feel, though, that the interests of justice have been served in this case as our system of jurisprudence does not permit trial or punishment of irresponsible persons.

Donald was declared insane and denied a trial because he was found to be "not responsible," yet without a trial Donald was sentenced to life in prison. The rationale: he was insane. But was he ill or a criminal? If a criminal, he deserved a trial. If ill, he deserved treatment. Donald received neither.

What Donald did experience was punishment far greater than if he had been tried for two murders and found guilty. Donald was committed to twenty-two years of torture and horror in one of the most notorious "hospitals" in the world.

When Donald arrived at Farview State Hospital, it was a place so much worse than any prison. Farview was called a "hellhole" by the inmates and later by the governor of Pennsylvania, the attorney general, and historians.

The History of Farview

When the cornerstone was laid for the Farview State Hospital in July of 1909, Dr. Charles C. Wagner, then superintendent of the State Hospital for the Insane at Binghamton, said as part of his remarks:

> If there were places of this kind available, there would be no longer any excuse for the deplorable practice of placing the insane even temporarily in common jails where, often, regardless of sex or mental disturbance they are grossly ill-treated. . . . Concentrated effort on behalf of the individual patient will be the watchword of the future. . . .

> [All the facilities here will] help banish the idea
> of prison bars and . . . make an environment that
> tends to aid in the recovery of the patient.

Located in Waymart, Pennsylvania, just outside Scranton, Farview State Hospital was immense, covering 1,345 acres. In 1947 Farview had an inmate population of 1,098 and 110 guards. By 1975, Farview had 1,300 inmates and 500 employees including 244 guards, making it the largest employer in Wayne County.

The true story of what happened at Farview emerged in 1976, the year following Donald's release. Wendell Rawls, Jr., and Acel Moore, senior reporters for the *Philadelphia Inquirer,* conducted an investigation into Farview. Their interest in the hospital came about because of a phone call to the newspaper by a former inmate at Farview who alleged that some patients at Farview had been murdered by guards.

Rawls and Moore took the man's story and began to investigate. They spent three months looking into Farview and interviewing about 200 people who corroborated what had happened inside Farview. Rawls and Moore discovered that in the Farview State Hospital from the 1940s into the 1970s, there were regular beatings, various forms of sexual and physical abuse, torture, and starvation, and, as reported, guards had murdered patients. The investigation disclosed that Farview was not a hospital. Rather, it was, according to Rawls, "a warehouse for an odd assortment of inmates—some criminal, some insane, some neither." And constant criminal activity implicated every level of the staff.

The initial series of newspaper articles was published in June and July of 1976 in the *Philadelphia Inquirer.* Rawls later wrote that none of the reported facts were questioned. In 1977 Rawls and Moore won the Pulitzer Local Reporting Award for their series on Farview State Hospital.

In 1976 a Pennsylvania grand jury was convened in response to the *Philadelphia Inquirer* series. The report of the grand jury confirmed all of the circumstances reported in the newspaper series and further stated that the conditions described, and the specific kinds of torture, beatings, human cockfights, sexual abuse, deprivation, medical neglect, and general mishandling of inmates was found to be true and widespread throughout the institution.

In 1980 Wendell Rawls published a book about Farview called *Cold Storage*. His book-length version of the investigation and the crimes at Farview describes in painful detail the zombielike prisoners, the sadistic guards, the starvation, malpractice, and murder.

Donald at Farview

There was no treatment and no medical care at Farview. It was a warehouse and worse; it was a torture chamber for most and a mortuary for some. There were no psychiatrists or therapists, although most patients did receive medications.

According to attorneys Josh Goldblum and Roy Diamond, who later helped to facilitate Donald's release as part of the Prison Research Council program, the most frequently administered medications at Farview were Prolixin and Haldol. Haldol is a second-generation form of phenothiazine known by the brand name Thorazine. Haldol and Prolixin could alleviate the symptoms of hallucination, delusion, and agitation, but they have side effects that include Parkinson's-like paralysis and clusters of painful and embarrassing involuntary movements called "tardive dyskinesia." Patients on normal doses of the medication would experience rapid jerking, twitches, lizard-like tongue thrusting, and spastic movements of their limbs.

At Farview these medications were used at double, triple, and quadruple doses to keep the patients living as zombies so the staff didn't have to keep an eye on them. As one of the guards, who was depicted in *Cold Storage,* explained, treatment was "a needle full of juice" or some Thorazine or Mellaril pills. Difficult patients received "a dose of Prolixin on top of Thorazine," causing them to look "like the fools they were."

Donald, like every new patient, would have been given those medications in his first years at Farview. But it is questionable how long he was maintained on this drug regimen or if he learned to "cheek" his meds, that is, put them in his mouth but later throw them away or trade them to others who preferred to be numb.

Donald was, at least in the years leading up to his encounters with the Prison Research Council, organized in a way that suggests he was not heavily medicated. He was able, and had the motivation and energy, to write letters, do research, and engage in conversation with others.

If they were capable, inmates could work at Farview. Farview had a farm that raised vegetables and beef cows. A number of inmates participated in the farm work, but as Rawls and Moore discovered, most of the fresh vegetables and meat went to the guards to take home.

It is almost certain that Donald was sexually abused in those years. The sexual abuse was widespread. Patients were made to participate in sexual acts with each other for the guards' "entertainment." Possibly Donald may have participated as a way to gain protection or to negotiate release from other tortures. This might have allowed him to remain unmedicated and thereby maintain his mental acuity. In *Cold Storage,* the grand jury's final report discussed the sexual abuse at Farview:

> As in most institutions where men are confined
> for long periods of time, homosexuality occurred
> at Farview State Hospital. However, as with
> other aspects, homosexuality at Farview assumed

a bizarre status. . . . At Farview, homosexuality was widespread and rampant, including in its participation a number of guards and hospital personnel who have worked at Farview through the years. Witnesses appeared before us and repeatedly told of having to engage in sodomy and perverse homosexual acts in order to amuse and entertain guards.

So here was Donald, condemned to life imprisonment without hope of appeal, in a place where brutality, sadism, and despair were the norm and "treatment" consisted of beatings, drug overdoses, and sexual torture. Then, adding insult to horrific injury, Donald was mandated to pay for this "treatment" at Farview. In 1956 the State of Pennsylvania—using Mellon Bank as its trustee—took Donald's remaining cash and all of his VA benefits to pay for his "care."

Even though Donald was experiencing this horrific combination of beatings, rape, and torture, he was able to maintain a level of psychic organization and enough emotional coherence to allow him to make his case when he found the expert who would begin the process of his liberation.

CHAPTER ELEVEN

Unveiling the Myth
of Thomas Szasz

Over the years—before and after Donald was in my life—I worked in human services and mental health programs. I knew the history and the public policies that drove changes in mental health programs.

In the 1970s, through a combination of medical advances and litigation inspired by the civil rights movement, the United States began the deinstitutionalization of the chronically mentally ill. This meant opening up psychiatric institutions to release hundreds of thousands of patients to the community.

One of the key factors that began the move toward deinstitutionalization was the discovery of the drug Thorazine. Prior to Thorazine, there was no chemical way to treat the symptoms of schizophrenia. The voices, delusions, and constant internal stimuli could not be abated.

When I worked in community education programs, one of my jobs was to help family and community members better understand the experience of mental illness. We'd begin each session with an opening exercise that was intended to simulate the experience of schizophrenia. It begins by asking participants to work on a simple task like a jigsaw puzzle or easy crossword. While they are doing the task, the leader turns on several different radios placed around the room—each one tuned to a different station. There is a confusion of sounds and music. One of the leaders also changes the lighting, randomly turning lights on and off so that the room is alternately dimmed and brightened.

While all of this is going on, the participants have to continue their task. And as they begin to struggle to pay attention, the leader moves through the group and whispers to participants one at a time, "You look like shit," "No one cares what you think," or "These people hate you." This experience is, after a few minutes, unnerving at best, and yet it is only a fair approximation of what persistent, unscreened stimuli are like for a person with schizophrenia.

But Thorazine, originally used to treat allergies, was found to make the noise and voices stop. Unfortunately, it also made people twitch, stare, shake—similar to Prolixin and Haldol— and make uncontrolled thrusting movements with their tongues. This tragic and permanent neurological side effect is called tardive dyskinesia.

But in its way, and in its time, it was a breakthrough. It meant people with schizophrenia did not need to be physically restrained, and they could live outside hospitals. That also meant taxpayers did not have to spend millions of dollars maintaining patients in hospitals. So, with the practice of deinstitutionalization, the heavily medicated— and critically unprepared—mentally ill came into the community.

Thomas Szasz, one of the most prolific and challenging writers on the subject of mental illness, rejected the term "deinstitutionalization." Szasz, a psychiatrist, insisted that the correct term for what happened as mental institutions began to shut down was "trans-institutionalization" because, he maintained, the institutions remained, but new legal structures and chemical restraints had replaced the hospital's bars and chains.

I first read Thomas Szasz's work as a graduate student at Towson State University in Baltimore. Our professor of rhetoric, Richard Vatz, had studied with Szasz in Syracuse, New York, and the book he assigned, *The Myth of Mental Illness,* was the second of Szasz's thirty-five books. In this landmark best seller, Szasz, then a young professor, made a compelling and revolutionary case that mental illness was a metaphor, and the medical model was not only wrong, it was unconstitutional. Szasz risked his career by issuing this challenge to the basic model of mental illness. The writings of Thomas Szasz became among the most hotly debated in psychiatry, linguistics, and sociology.

I remember thinking as I read *The Myth of Mental Illness, This man doesn't understand that people need help.* I thought Szasz must be a cold intellectual who had more concern for linguistic rules than for human beings.

So I knew Thomas Szasz was brilliant but controversial, and he had the ability to think and write in one of the most confusing intersections of medicine, language, and ethics. I also knew that he paid a huge price for his words. Within a year of the publication of *The Myth of Mental Illness,* the New York State Department of Mental Hygiene demanded that Szasz be dismissed from his tenured university position. And even though he was the most published psychiatrist in the world, Szasz's research was never published in the *Journal of the American Psychiatric Association.*

★ ★ ★

When Donald died in 1996, in a state of acute dementia, he had few possessions. My sister Gloria had packed up his things and stored the boxes in her garage. In the spring of 1999 when the *Times Union* editor questioned Donald's past, I wrote to my sister in Florida and asked her if she still had any of Donald's papers.

A few months later, I arrived home from work one evening and found a fat manila envelope from Gloria in that day's mail. As I stood in the kitchen talking to my husband, I opened the envelope from Gloria, saying things like "This is great. She found Donald's papers. Oh, cool, here's his driver's license, Social Security card, and veteran's ID card." I was thrilled; I knew these cards with their all-important numbers would save me time in my research. Still wearing my coat, I continued to read and flipped to the back of the pile where I saw a page of letterhead from Farview State Hospital.

I began to read the letter and saw that it referenced some lawyers. I knew Donald had been engaged in a legal battle for his release for years. Now I had the documentation. I was turning the pages one by one as I told my husband what I was reading. "This is great. I've got his discharge here." And then, as I looked at the last page, I fell silent. I couldn't believe my eyes.

"Oh my God," I said, shaking the papers. "Oh my God; it was Szasz." It was indeed the renowned Thomas Szasz whose psychiatric intervention had led to Donald's release.

★ ★ ★

In November of 1999, I take my Subaru Legacy and drive from Albany to Syracuse, three hours across New York State. I have never been to Syracuse and don't want to be late for my appointment with the most controversial psychiatrist in the world.

I am nervous, but I am prepared for our discussion. I reread *The Myth of Mental Illness* and looked at the website created by Szasz's disciples. It isn't just his stance on mental illness that has me rattled. I am afraid of what Szasz will be like. After all, he has taken on the field of psychiatry and isn't afraid to go up against the State of New York or the Supreme Court. What am I in for?

Even after missing one exit and making a couple of wrong turns, I make it to the suburbs of Syracuse well before my appointment. I find the Szasz house and drive past it to the end of the block. It is a wooded, upper-middle-class neighborhood, but there are no sidewalks, only long driveways. I can't pull over and wait, so I have to pull into his driveway.

"Okay," I tell myself, "I can stay a few minutes and then leave." I don't want to waste this man's time. After all, I remind myself, Thomas Szasz is a physician, psychiatrist, analyst, and linguist who has written thirty-five scholarly books. My nerves are jumping, and my insecurities are bumping into each other.

Gravel crunches as I drive into the driveway. I take a deep breath and walk to the carved-wood front door. I gulp and ring the bell. The door opens immediately and a small, white-haired man beams at me.

"Oh, Mrs. Cameron, I'm glad you came early. I've been waiting all day to talk with you." Here is another eighty-year-old man with a story he can't wait to tell.

We sit in a small, comfortable den off the living room. I notice the books and artwork, a collection of African masks, and two tall ceramic jars that held a dozen carved and decorated walking sticks. I sit in a deep leather chair and lay my files and writing tablet on my lap. Szasz sits across from me and explains that he'd finished his writing for the day at noon. He is still averaging about four hours a day of writing; the rest of his work is research and, of course, editing many articles and reviews for journals and magazines. This is a busy "retirement."

"You remember Donald?" I begin.

He smiles and says, "It was a long time ago, but he was one of the first cases. I was doing a lot of expert testimony work then, and he had written to me."

I explain that I'd read his books and studied with Richard Vatz in Baltimore, and I need to ask him about some of his ideas to get a better understanding of Donald's case. I tell him that I know about what had happened to Donald before Farview and . . .

"He wasn't mentally ill," Szasz interrupts.

"Well, yes, that's what I'm trying to understand."

Szasz looks at me and smiles. "There's no such thing as mental illness," he says. And I laugh. This is going to be good.

I ask him if there was an early experience that had influenced him, that had turned him against psychiatry.

"Everyone asks that, but no; I was young, maybe nine years old, no older than twelve, when I began to think about the language of medicine and how it can control people." He describes the parallel of how religion is used to control people and how some people let religion sweep them into a state that can allow a government to take over their lives.

"I grew up in Austria, you know, and being exposed to Nazism shaped my interest in language. There is a part in all of us that wants something or someone to take care of us; we want to close our eyes and collapse into being taken care of. A religion will do that; a government will do that if we keep our eyes closed. We will gladly give up our rights if someone will take care of us."

Szasz goes on talking about religion and psychiatry. "It's not an atheist who can challenge the church."

"Well then," I ask him, "Who, in addition to you, can challenge psychiatry?"

"It will be those like Jung and Laing and those thinkers. The state can't challenge psychiatry; that's like an atheist challenging the pope. Remember, it took another religious man—Martin Luther—to challenge the papacy. And you have to remember, the concept of mental illness undermines personal responsibility, and that is the ground on which all free political institutions rest."

I ask him about people with schizophrenia. "Don't you believe these people suffer?"

"Diane, this is what most people misunderstand about my work, and most people don't actually read my work; they just know the titles of my books. People suffer terribly, and they have all manner of difficulties with living. Some have physical problems that require medicine, and some just let go and let themselves cross over."

I ask him about this "letting go."

"There is a point in a schizophrenic's life, and most of them can describe it, when they decide to let themselves cross over, to allow their thoughts to run them."

"Is it a kind of allowing; they allow themselves?"

"Yes," he says, "people allow themselves to slip away; they commit schizophrenia. We all know those times of just allowing ourselves to slip away, allowing our thinking to slip; well, schizophrenics stay there when the rest of us come back. There is tiredness in that; it's a kind of giving up. And yes, they suffer, but there is choice—volition. It is truly awful, but it's not illness."

"What do we do then, as a society, with someone who 'commits schizophrenia' and then commits a crime, a murder, like Donald?"

Szasz takes a deep breath before responding. I can tell that he's answered this question many times. "People who commit a crime should be arrested and charged, allowed to say their piece, stand trial, and be sentenced. They might be sentenced to a prison for people with special problems, just as there are facilities in prison for people with cardiac problems or diabetes. It would be their choice, though. They would make the choice: regular prison or special prison, but not hospital. They could be offered medicines, but let's not pretend it's a hospital.

"One of my questions is," he says, leaning forward, "is it a job for physicians to lock people up and deprive them of liberty? Think about what prisons do. They state their case explicitly: You serve this much time and then you get out. We don't ask prisoners to prove they are no longer dangerous after they have served their time. We release dangerous people all the time. That's our legal system. But in a mental institution, you can be retained forever and you have to prove your sanity, an almost impossible situation, especially since being in a mental hospital means you are mentally ill."

I ask him about Donald and how he helped him. "Did it trouble you that he had killed his wife and mother-in-law?"

"That he killed his intimate family," Szasz says, laughing. "You have to remember these are two of the most imagined crimes that human beings have: killing your spouse and killing your mother-in-law."

Szasz continues, "We say that killing a family member is . . . we use this word 'unimaginable,' but that's not true. These are, in fact, very imaginable, among the most imaginable crimes. Few of us ever imagine killing a complete stranger, but we do have thoughts or impulses to kill within the family: a child, parent, spouse, or sibling. That is why we have the story of Abraham and Isaac and the story of Cain and Abel.

"These are not unimaginable; they are the most imaginable. That is why we have a taboo against them; we are especially angered when a member of society or a community breaks our secret taboo and does what we have most imagined. The taboo is so strong that we have to make them a special horror, the worst of criminals, a mother killing her children, a man killing his wife, and the biggest: killing your mother-in-law. That particular murder fantasy is so strong in our culture that we have created humor about it: the cartoons, jokes, we have that comedian . . ."

"Rodney Dangerfield?" I prompt.

"Yes," Szasz continues, "his whole act is about how he wants to kill his mother-in-law. But Donald Watkins did it—he actually did it—and that is part of his crime: He surfaced the taboo; he made a secret fantasy that is prevalent in our culture and society real and visible."

"So that's why he has to be insane?" I ask.

"Yes; most normal people cannot imagine killing a bank teller, but most normal people have at some time felt enough rage to fantasize the death of an in-law, a spouse, or a child. What makes it so offensive to us is the fact that these so-called mentally ill people commit the crimes we *can* imagine. They commit not the unimaginable crime, but the most imaginable.

"We have such intolerance for that part of ourselves that we must distance ourselves as far as possible from those who act on what we call *unimaginable* but what is actually *unthinkable*. Those are the killings we most want to punish people for. We do not want to think about these impulses that we all have; they are so socially unacceptable, so we have special names and special punishments for those who make us think about them. These crimes are taboo for the stabilization of family and community. That your Donald did it was offensive to everyone who has wished it and repressed it.

"Think about another one," he says. "Also at St. Elizabeths. Remember John Hinckley? Lots of people wanted to kill Reagan, many would have liked to, but they were horrified when someone tried to. And 'going postal' is about killing your coworkers." He pauses and then laughs. "Who hasn't wished their annoying coworker would disappear on a Monday?"

I think of Andrew Goldstein, the young mental patient in New York City who, in 1999, pushed a young woman, Kendra Webdale, under a subway train. "Kendra's Law," I say to Szasz, "the man in the subway?"

"Yes." He laughs again, nodding at me like teacher to pupil. "Think of the busy, grimy, hot subway, everyone crowding. Who hasn't thought of shoving someone out of the way, shoving the person in front of him? People in the subway stand and stare at the tracks, they imagine falling in, jumping in, being pushed. It makes us fear for our own shallow sanity, for the thinness of the line that separates us from him."

"We imagine," I say, "but he acted."

"Another one," Szasz says, nodding excitedly. "Ezra Pound was also at St. Elizabeths. Pound was the most famous prisoner there. He made antiwar broadcasts, and he pissed off Roosevelt, so the government and his wife committed him. It was a social offense; being antiwar in World War II meant you had to be crazy. It was a crime against a particular social structure. He got twenty years for having a disturbing opinion.

"We use the language of the mentally ill against them," he says, shifting now to another idea, and I can see the thoughts sweep across his small face. "When Kaczynski, the Unabomber, said he didn't want to be tried as mentally ill, that very appeal was used as proof of his mental illness. You can't win. We don't make criminals prove their innocence; we presume that. But we make the mentally ill prove their sanity. We deny them their rights. It's a civil rights issue.

"You have to know history and literature," he tells me. "Before there is psychiatry, before there is mental illness, there is a kind of family problem that's described in *Macbeth*, *King Lear*, and *Hamlet*. These are problems of incompetence, senility, and a dangerous young man who believes his mother is a killer. Do you know that Freud and many other people have analyzed Hamlet as a schizophrenic—because he can't decide? Well, how are you supposed to feel if you think your mother killed your father? What kind of mental state are you supposed to be in? Are you supposed to be tranquil and happy? These are family problems, not mental illness."

I can hear the professor in me at work. "But these family problems disrupted society, and so to take care of these family problems, especially as the rural became urban, we saw the creation of the private mental hospitals. It was good business. The trade in lunacy was a business."

"Diane," he says, leaning back so I know our talk is coming to a close, "is every form of suffering an illness?"

I start to stand up. We have talked for more than two hours. I have scribbled notes all over the writing tablet in front of me. "You have helped me so much; I want to talk to you again. May I come back?" I ask.

"Yes," he says and quickly stands.

He walks me to the front door and shakes my hand. As I step onto the porch, I thank him again for this afternoon.

Szasz smiles and nods. "I'm going to be eighty in the spring; you can come to my birthday party."

Driving back to Albany, I think about Donald and how hard he worked to get out of Farview, and how he had lived in that intersection of crime and mental illness Szasz talked about. And I think of all that Thomas Szasz has suffered over the years, his passion for his work, and how much rejection he has experienced—and everyone called him crazy.

CHAPTER TWELVE

Getting Help and Getting Home Again

After reading Rawls's *Cold Storage,* I knew Thomas Szasz was frighteningly correct about one thing: Donald would have been better off in prison. The "patients" at Farview had suffered violations not only to their civil rights but to their bodies and psyches as well.

For years, as my research continued, I was working in human services and writing a newspaper column. Occasionally I would pull out my Donald files and wonder if I could find something more that might solve the puzzle of Donald Watkins.

I could trace Donald's path from China to St. Elizabeths, then home to the murders, and then to Farview. Also, I'd made the connection to Szasz. I knew that Szasz's testimony had been a central factor and could see in those old documents that two attorneys, Diamond and Goldblum, had done the legal work on Donald's discharge, but there the path stopped.

Every year when I'd pick up the files and go through Donald's papers again, I'd try to find the attorneys. I had called the University of Pennsylvania. They had no record. I'd looked at Penn's website. Nothing there. I tried directory assistance for Greater Philadelphia. No luck.

Then, on a late November day in 2003, sitting at work, I started thinking about the attorneys again. I was taking a writing class then at SUNY Albany with the poet Ed Sanders, who had written a book about Charles Manson and the Manson Family. His class was called Investigative Poetry and Prose, and I was admitted to the class based on a piece I had written about Donald and the murders. I was taking my files to Ed's class that night, so I pulled out the 1975 correspondence between Szasz and the two attorneys.

I typed the names into Google, and there at the top of the list I saw a Joshua Goldblum listed as part of a law firm near Philadelphia. It was called Family Collaborative Law Affiliates. *Close enough,* I thought. I scanned the website for a fax number and composed a brief note:

> Dear Mr. Goldblum, I am attaching a document that I hope will bring back memories of a wonderful service you performed many years ago. In 1975 you assisted Donald K. Watkins in his liberation from Farview State Hospital with the help of Doctor Thomas Szasz.

I added that I had been trying for years to find the attorneys who helped Donald and asked if I could talk to him. I faxed the note and a copy of the 1975 Szasz letter.

About twenty minutes later the receptionist at my office called me. "Diane, you have a call, Mr. Goldblum, I think, from Philadelphia."

After all this time, and just like that.

I spoke to Josh that day and he told me, yes, he remembered Donald. And when he got my fax, he faxed it over to Roy Diamond. They were still friends. Josh asked me what had happened to Donald, and I explained that he'd moved back to Western Pennsylvania after Farview, then met my mother, and they'd had a romance and good marriage.

"I am so glad," he said, "that Donald got a life after Farview."

I thanked him. "You saved Donald's life, you know."

"Oh, I don't know. We were pretty young," he said and laughed.

I asked if I could come to talk to him and maybe meet Roy Diamond as well.

"Sure, email me some dates; I'll check with Roy."

★ ★ ★

In late January of 2004, I take an afternoon train to New York City and transfer to the train to Philadelphia. The Chestnut Hill Inn is shabbily chic, and as the Internet description says, it "overlooked cobblestone streets and shopping." I spend the afternoon strolling up Germantown Avenue looking at clothes in fancy boutiques and art in small galleries.

The next morning I go downstairs for breakfast. On the small elevator a young woman, perhaps in her late twenties, gets on with an older woman. They ask if my room is hot or cold. They mention they have an infant with them so they want to keep their room very warm. The baby is three months old, they say, and I ask, "Is this the baby's first trip?"

"Yes," the young mom says with a smile. The woman had come from New York for a job interview and her parents had come from New Jersey to watch the baby while she had her meeting. I think about that—parents who would come and help you—and it all seems so normal.

A small sitting room off the hotel lobby has been set up with coffee and pastries. I have coffee and a roll, but my stomach aches. I am nervous again. *Could I leave now?* I page through *USA Today.* I hear the front door open and then I hear voices at the front desk: "We're meeting someone here." They are here.

"Are you Diane?" We are all smiling. "I can't believe you came all this way," Roy says.

"I can't believe you guys are real," I reply. "For years you two have been names on a piece of paper." We step outside and walk up Germantown Avenue to a local cafe.

Both men look to be in their early fifties. Josh has thinning gray hair and big, wire-rimmed glasses. Roy's hair also has some gray, but it is close-cropped. He is wearing a canvas Carhartt parka.

The sidewalk is narrow, so I walk ahead of the two men and have to keep turning around to talk to them. I tell them how much I like Chestnut Hill and have spent the day before walking around the neighborhood. I ask if both of them had grown up in Philadelphia. Yes, both of them had.

We find a table at Rollers, a small, casual café. It is cozy and brightly painted. We hang our coats.

The restaurant tables are each set for two customers, so we sit across two tables. Roy sits across from me; Josh sits to my right. They are talking to each other as I settle myself, pulling out my Prison Research Council file.

"Did you meet *in* law school?" I ask.

"No," Roy says, "we met at summer camp in the Poconos when we were kids. We saw each other there over several summers but reconnected in law school."

Roy had studied philosophy as an undergraduate, and Josh was a psychology major. They say they went to law school because they didn't know what to do after college, and their parents were relieved they got into graduate school.

I ask them how they had come to work on the Prison Research Council. Roy explains, "The University of

Pennsylvania had gotten a grant for a prison program. The Law Enforcement Assistance Agency put up some money for the project. It was only supposed to be for a couple of years, but there was enough money for a few law students for a summer program."

Roy doesn't remember how he found out about the project; maybe it was on a bulletin board, he says. Josh says that he had hoped to get an internship with a big firm. He'd noticed that was what other law students did, but he didn't get one. Then Roy told him about the Prison Research Council, so he signed on.

There was money to hire two students to work with prisoners and two to work with mental patients. Josh and Roy were the team chosen to work with mental patients.

"Basically," Roy says, "we had an empty office and a big box of files. They were files of the people who had written to the Prison Research Council for help. We went through the files and selected some cases. Then we wrote to the inmates to see if they still wanted help."

Roy talks about his memories of that time and the summer project. "We both came to the project as kind of misfits. We were in law school, but we didn't really know what we wanted to do, and this summer project, it set a course for us."

Both men finished law school at Penn and then became what they call "advocate lawyers." Josh had worked for several years as a public defender, and now he works in family law.

"I help people get divorced without killing each other," he describes. "I also do a lot of bankruptcy work, so I see the lives of people in poverty."

"Look at what we do now," Josh says. Roy nods. "Roy develops housing and real estate for nonprofit organizations, and he is still an advocate for people with disabilities."

"I have a son with autism," Roy says, looking at me. "I'm still living this. I have to care about what happens to people in institutions."

"The alternative," Josh says, "would be doing corporate work and then once a year doing some pro bono cases to feel good about something."

At one point, laughing, they are reminding each other—and telling me—how accidental it seemed at the time, but they both knew they wanted to do something good and that summer law project showed them a way that law could be used to do good. It turned out that helping inmates had the unexpected benefit of shaping their later careers.

Both had felt, they say, "like schmucks and misfits" in law school. "Other guys were getting internships with big firms and going to corporate jobs. I didn't even know that was why people went to Penn," Josh says. "We ended up on the project by kind of bumbling around and then this good stuff happens."

He points at the file in front of me. Smiling, I say, "If you do good, good will happen."

"Yes," Josh says, "that's what I tell my kids."

We have more coffee and keep talking. I ask them, "Was there ever a moment when you were working with Donald that you thought, 'This guy killed his wife and her mother'?"

Roy says, "Yeah, we used to talk about that, but we knew our role was the process, to apply the law."

"Had everyone in Farview committed crimes?"

"No, most of them were civil commitments; in those days it only took one doctor to get you locked up. But these men had the right to psychiatric evaluations and to have their cases reviewed."

"Well, yeah," Josh says, "but after we saw Farview and what a hole it was—smelly, dirty, no services—our goal was to try to get people out of there and into less restrictive settings."

The idea of taking on a case like Donald's was to test the question of whether psychiatric commitment was indefinite.

"Donald had been declared insane and was committed for insanity. At Farview most of the patients were committed indefinitely. Later," Roy says, "it was decided that indefinite commitment was unconstitutional, but that was later.

"The game plan for us, for Donald, was to get a psychiatric review," he continues, "and as Szasz says in his report, Donald was no longer insane, and he never received any kind of treatment, so by those terms he should not be kept."

"In most cases," Josh interjects, "we were trying to get people moved to less restrictive settings, to places where their families could visit them. Farview was in the middle of nowhere. Families didn't visit, so no one saw what was going on. Our thought was that by getting people moved to Norristown or some place closer to transportation, then their families could advocate for them."

"Farview," Roy adds, "had no psychiatrist, only a country doctor. And the guards."

I ask if they remember other things about Donald.

"Oh yeah, I remember Don," Josh says, turning to Roy. "He told us all about being in China, the ship he went over on, and how they went up the river to some old city. Don was smart; he knew his rights; he'd done his reading." Roy nods.

"He sent us money, too," Josh says, turning to Roy and then back to me. "He sent us a thousand dollars a couple of years after he got out, but being young and idealistic"—he looks at Roy, and they both roll their eyes and laugh—"we wouldn't take it and sent it back to him. I think he sent some University of Pennsylvania framed mirrors for the law school clinic.

"You know, the system had so little structure and so little order that we got in under the radar," Josh laughs. "It wasn't a strategy or anything; we just didn't know any better."

They had asked the records clerk at Farview for Donald's medical records and they got them.

"You learn to ask people in these lowly, no-respect jobs to help you, and if you're nice to them, they'll want to help you. At Farview they didn't know what to make of us asking to meet with patients, and they didn't care. We were just lowly law students," Roy says. "Yeah, we were kids."

"Donald was the one who orchestrated it," Josh says. "His was one of the letters in the files when we joined the law project; he'd written several times. He knew about Szasz."

That surprises me. Donald had "orchestrated it." He had done the work of finding Szasz and finding the law project. This speaks of his intelligence, and it suggests something else, some internal quality of Donald's. Is it resilience, determination, an insistence on survival?

"He was something; you could see that military thing in him. He had this great posture—he was a little stiff," Josh says.

"Everyone was diagnosed schizophrenic in those days," Roy adds. "It was the most common diagnosis. And it made it simple, too, because it didn't take much refinement; a diagnosis of schizophrenia allowed everyone to be given Haldol and Prolixin. They were the drugs. Everybody at Farview got them, and they kept the patients heavily medicated."

We leave the deli at one o'clock. On the sidewalk, I hug Josh and Roy, smiling and thinking to myself that the two "important attorneys" I've been looking for turned out to be my age, and they are really nice, middle-aged guys making middle-class lives in a Philadelphia suburb. They'd changed Donald's life, and he'd shaped their careers; now they have helped me as well.

Donald Meets Josh and Roy at Farview—1975

The guard came to tell him that he had visitors. They were not nice to him, nor were they mean. He was just another one, another crazy guy. This one was smart, though. He talked to the guards sometimes, the ones who were going to college. He wrote letters and had piles of books in his cell. He was unpredictable and had a strange look in his eye.

He brushed his hair straight back. It was light brown, but some gray was showing on the sides now. He put on an old, tweed sports jacket that came from the used clothes that the guards' wives sent sometimes. He gathered some papers from the shelf in his cell. Upon leaving the cell with the guards, he looked like he could be their supervisor—tall, lean, and not smiling.

In the warden's office he greeted the secretary by name. She said good morning and straightened slightly. She pointed to the small room off the reception area. Two young men rose when he entered.

Introductions were made and, still not smiling, he put his files on the small desk. He pulled some papers from one of the files. Here was a Marine discharge, a Social Security form, and newspaper clippings from years ago. The young men were hesitant. They smiled and explained that this was a project. They were helping prisoners, people in his situation. They did not use the words "patient," "mental," or "insane." They were new at this, still students, their voices unsure.

"Twenty-two years," Donald said. "An examination will confirm I am sane and can petition for release."

They did not discuss the murders or his wife. They did not ask him if he had been abused. He did not tell them about the beatings and fights at night or about the men who disappear.

He was organized. These were his papers and files. From another file, he took a thick pile of letters. They could see the United States Marines insignia, the globe and anchor at the top of each page. It looked like years of letters, and he turned each one over, explaining each step he had taken, each request, and each petition.

They interrupted him. "Do you want to see a psychiatrist? We can request that; you have that right."

He didn't look at them but moved his papers into new piles. From the manila folder he brought out more letters; these had the logo of the State University of New York, from a doctor in Syracuse. "He is the one; he's the expert on this kind of thing."

They looked at the letters. "Yeah, I've heard that name," one said.

"Okay, we can ask him. Syracuse is not too far, about two hours, right?" said the other. "We can ask him to see you and give a report to us."

His hands stopped moving. One hand rested on the papers, and the other gripped the side of the table. His lips were pressed tightly together.

"We'll figure this out; you have rights. We'll help you get the paperwork and then apply to have you see this doctor."

He was staring at them now, through them. They looked around and back. "Mr. Watkins?"

He saw they were still sitting, looking at him, holding the papers with his name on them; they had other papers, other names. One of them stood and said, "It was good to meet you, Mr. Watkins."

"Yes," he said, "I have more of these, you could make copies." He slid newspaper clippings about the murders toward them. Then he stood and extended a hand, his jaw tight. "I will pay you," he said.

"No, no, this is a project; the state is paying us to help you."

A silence. The law students were both standing now. Then he laughed.

"The state is paying?" He laughed again. "The state is paying to help me out of this?" He gestured to the reception area where the guards were waiting.

The young men laughed nervously. "Yes, well, we'll write to that doctor and we'll know something when we come back next month."

From Farview to the VA and Home Again

Josh and Roy, following Donald's guidance, contacted Thomas Szasz and asked him to see Donald and provide expert testimony on the civil rights and legal issues pertaining to Donald's case. It was a perfect case for an advocate like Szasz. There had been no trial; two local doctors and Donald's own defense attorney had declared him insane.

Josh and Roy took the report from Thomas Szasz and submitted a writ of habeas corpus in the Wayne County Court effecting the discharge of Donald K. Watkins from Farview State Hospital. In two days, the paperwork was complete, and Donald was released. His discharge included a transfer to the Leach Farm VA Hospital in Pittsburgh. His admission there was a voluntary and temporary measure to help him make the transition back into society—a society greatly changed in twenty-two years. Donald was suddenly—and frightfully—a free man.

Donald at the VA after Farview—1975

He walked to the main office from his room on the first floor. He was nervous about being outside but also excited, a little hungry, and some other feeling he couldn't name. The people at the hospital told him that he should have a place to stay for a couple of nights. "You'll be confused at first, but that will go away," they'd said.

But the people at the VA had been good, nice. When he'd come in to talk, they'd called him "Marine Watkins" and smiled at him. The young man at the desk, no older than a kid, really, had said, "So, China, huh? Boy, I bet that was something. When was that?" He looked at Donald's papers. "Wow, that was before the war; you really saw some stuff, didn't you?"

The young man hadn't asked about Farview and hadn't talked about that other hospital. Here he was a Marine and a veteran; they had some order here, you could see that; they knew how to run a place the military way.

The young man had given him a laminated card and said, "This is for shopping at the PX and for the liquor store; that's in a separate part of the PX now, and you'll need this card for the doctor and all that, too." He lowered his eyes when he mentioned the doctor.

He picked up the card and the pile of papers the young man slid toward him.

"All right then," he said, and then didn't know what else to say.

The young man looked at him and said, "Do you have a car, sir?"

He looked back at the young man's face, hesitated, and then said, "No, I do not; I came on the bus." He started stacking his papers again and tapping them into a neat pile.

The young man nodded slowly and said, "China, wow." Then it looked as if a thought had come to him. "Uh, sir, can you wait here a minute? I'll be right back, okay?" He left the room.

He was gone for a few minutes then came back with a woman. She appeared to be in her forties, but he couldn't really say.

"This is Andrea; she's a social worker here, and I was thinking that since you didn't have a car, and you came from, I mean the bus trip was pretty long and all"—he hesitated, looking at the woman and then back—"you can stay at a motel near here, a really nice place. We have vouchers; it's all paid for and everything." His voice began to trail off as he looked at the woman again.

"I have money; I have my own money, and I don't need . . ." he said as he began to stand.

"Excuse me, Marine," the woman said, stepping closer. "This is your VA benefit, it's part of your discharge package—this is for all veterans, nothing special. This is a veteran's benefit, and we'd like to make the standard reservation for you. And I think," she said as she looked at the young man again, "I think two nights will be enough, and that way you'll get to know us here and you'll want some time to see the PX and get yourself some things." She smiled. "Yes, that's what I think." She handed a paper to the young man, who nodded. "An honor to meet you, sir. Thank you for your service to our country." She hesitated, then nodded at the young man again and walked out of the room.

He sat down again. "My discharge was honorable; I have the paperwork here, I got that in 1946, and I—"

"That's okay, sir, we have all your paperwork right here." The young man tapped the pile of papers again. "These are your copies; we have a whole set, too." He smiled. "The motel is just up the road, not far at all. You can probably . . ." He hesitated again. "You know what, I think the man who drives the van is up front right now, sir. I'll go and arrange your transportation."

"But, I—"

"No sir, standard issue, SOP, sir; this is standard operating procedure."

★ ★ ★

When I think back over my conversation with Josh and Roy, two feelings emerge. One is gratitude for those two young law students, naive by their own description but committed to the law and to doing good. But I also feel worry, remembering how Josh and Roy described Donald as "a little stiff." Was that rigidity or resilience? Or was it fear?

Now that we know what went on at Farview, how brutal the beatings and how sadistic the guards' behavior, I realize the risk that Donald took in asking to meet with Josh and Roy. I often think about how much fear Donald felt for most of his life. He was traumatized in China, then the murders, and then he was abused for many years as a mental patient. But in the midst of that is another part of Donald that attracts me. There was a constant in Donald's personality that acted as a tropism, always turning toward survival. He had the quality that today we call resilience. It led to his survival each time. But it had costs—big costs—for Donald and for the people around him.

CHAPTER THIRTEEN

Donald Crosses the Line

I was in my thirties and newly divorced when my mother met Donald. Conversations with my women friends were all about whether love and happiness were really possible. And here was my mother, beginning a new romance in her seventies.

When I talked to my mother on the phone, I could hear that she and Donald were happy. They were doing the things she liked: going to movies and out to dinner, and having sex. Hearing that was like being a kid and not wanting to know that your parents had sex, but now I was learning that my seventy-six-year-old mother and her eighty-year-old husband still did "it." Every day.

My mother had something else that my friends and I wanted. She had a flexible and supportive marriage. Donald had spent many years alone after he came out of Farview. He was probably an introvert by nature, but certainly being away from society for so long did nothing for his people skills. And, of course, he couldn't really participate in the small talk that happens between older people. I mean, what could he say when someone asked, "So, Donald, what did you do before retirement?"

Florence was the opposite. She hated to go anywhere alone, preferring to gather up one of her children or a friend, even a stranger if necessary, to go to the movies or to a show. My mother had always been a lively and active woman. Her friends described her as "high-spirited," "energetic," and even "handsome." Those were, of course, euphemisms for what they didn't say: She wasn't pretty. That, I knew, had been a source of pain all my mother's life.

There was more to my mother's story. Florence was not the only child of my grandparents, Frank and Josephine Shermock. Before my mother was born, they had another daughter, Anna, who was blonde and pretty.

Anna died when she was four years old. There was a terrible accident; her dress had touched an open stove, and it caught on fire. She was badly burned and died at home from infection.

The loss of their little girl, their first child, changed my mother's parents. They couldn't cope. But Josephine was already pregnant with my mother. The timing was terrible. My mother lived in the shadow of Anna's death.

I knew about Anna when I was a little girl. I'd heard about the fire, and it was why we were always warned to stay away from matches, stoves, and candles. I knew that Anna's death had cost my mother her parents' love. But I didn't know until I was older how deep that wound truly was.

One day my mother and I were talking about the lasting impact of things parents say to their children. I was in therapy then and working through my own childhood leftovers, and I was trying to explain to my mother how her constant pressure had left me with big insecurities.

My mother said, yes, she understood that. She paused, looking very sad, and she said, "Grampa could be quite mean, you know. He hated it if I fussed with my hair or my clothes." She told me my grandfather would sneer at her if he caught her looking in a mirror, and he would say to her almost daily, "You can forget it; the pretty one died."

As a little girl and young woman, my mother was told by her father, "The pretty one died." I finally understood my mother's urgency that her own daughters must be attractive, and it explained her terrible ambivalence when we were.

Donald changed this. One day, sitting with Donald and waiting, as we often did for my perpetually late mother to finish dressing, I said, "What takes her so long?"

Donald said softly, "Well, your mother is such a beautiful woman."

The Accident—1992

He folded the newspaper in half and in half again and placed it neatly next to the magazines on the coffee table. He looked at his watch. She was still in the bathroom. He could hear the water running, and she was talking. To herself? To him? He couldn't tell.

He looked at his watch again. "Come on, Flo, we have to get going."

The water ran again, and then the toilet flushed. She was talking about something at a store, the store near the mall where they'd have lunch.

She came out of the bathroom and picked up her blouse from the chair in the dining area. She had painted on her lipstick, and her eyebrows were dark now, but her head was almost bare; a few strands of hair were damply laid across her skull. She picked up her handbag and a pile of coupons from the kitchen counter and moved them to the floor near the front door. She grimaced, holding her hip, as she straightened up. "Let's go see that new store after we eat," she was saying. Then she touched her head and laughed, putting her bags down again.

He was standing now, pulling on his suit jacket, smoothing his trousers, and he looked at his shoes. He moved to the kitchen counter, took the dish towel, and bent to wipe his shoe. The small bit of dirt wiped away easily. He hung the towel back on the handle of the refrigerator door and glanced up at the clock.

She was coming out of the bedroom now; her wig in place, she looked different, less strange. He smiled. She was smiling at him, picking up her bag. "Let's go, we have to go," she said, opening the apartment door and starting out. He began to follow her and then reached back around the door frame to flick off the kitchen light.

They walked slowly to the elevator. She was bent slightly, moving with careful steps. Her knees were bad; one was a new knee from surgery a few years ago, the other equally as bad now. They rode down to the first floor, then walked to the car in front of the building. She was talking as she walked. "I'll call Larry tonight; he can fix that little light in the bathroom. I don't know why it keeps going out; he can fix it and buy a new socket."

He was listening and walking upright, head high; he seemed like a tall man, but it was his posture that made him seem more than his five feet, eight inches. His thoughts were calm but not clear. *Lunch, we'll eat lunch, then something. We have to do something after lunch,* he thought. He couldn't remember the things she said. It was confusing to listen, but he tried. He liked her voice but didn't understand why she said so many things.

At the car, he walked ahead of her to open the passenger door. She smiled up at him, and he took her bag and fumbled with the coupons, reaching inside to put them on the dashboard in front of her seat. She held onto the door frame and lowered herself into the car, making a wincing grunt. Her hip hurt, too, more pain. She lifted her left leg into the car, and then with her hand helped place her right leg beside it. He reached to hand her the seat belt and waited until it was fastened, then he closed her door and quickly walked around to the driver's side.

Where are we going? he thought as he sat behind the wheel and turned the keys in his hands to find the ignition key. *Where were we going?*

She was talking about something else now, what a man on the news had said. Something about voting? He turned the key in the ignition, and the car started. He pressed the gas, but no movement, only a grinding. The brake. He reached down and released the emergency brake. Into reverse now; the car jolted. Back too fast, brake too hard. The car stalled.

"Damn," he muttered.

"Look where you're going," she said, not looking at him. "You have to turn and look. They say people like us, old people, never look; we have to get bigger mirrors. You have to look, you know."

He ignored her and started the car again. The car went into reverse easily this time, and they headed out of the driveway of the senior apartment complex. At the end of the driveway, he swung into traffic. A car close behind him honked as he cut in front.

She was looking in her purse now. "I had those coupons. Did I forget the coupons?" She was pulling things out of her bag.

At the bottom of the hill at a light, he pulled onto the four-lane road. For a moment he didn't feel his body; a blurry feeling, a fog came over him. *Cars too fast, too fast,* he thought.

Her voiced jabbed at him now. "Where are the coupons? We forgot them."

He was staring straight ahead, sitting forward too stiffly. He accelerated to thirty, then forty, then forty-five miles per hour.

Cars were behind him and moving to the left, passing. Some he saw, others went unnoticed.

"I forgot my coupons," she was saying, now clearly upset. "We have to go back, Don, turn the car around."

He felt a burning under his belt, and his hands tightened on the wheel.

"We have to go back." Her voice was high now.

He accelerated more. "We have to eat lunch . . . time for lunch," he said, not looking at her as he accelerated to fifty-five miles per hour. Cars were passing on the left. He began to drift left.

"There's the mall, there's the mall," she said, pointing right. "Oh Don, we can go here to eat, turn right, turn right, we can eat here." She pointed to a small strip center as they passed it.

His eyes were drawn to movement in the rearview mirror; there was a car there, closer to them. *How did that car get there? Who is . . .* And then there was a car on the left. *Why are they pushing? Who is following?*

"Shut up," he said. "Can you shut up and let me drive the car?"

She was talking more now as she reached for the dashboard and said, "Here are my coupons; I left them here. We can go to the mall, then eat."

He turned to look at her, and, turning back, he moved the steering wheel along with his gaze. They drifted into the left lane. A car honked loudly. "Bastard," he said.

Across the road, in the opposite lanes, cars and trucks were moving south to Pittsburgh. She was talking still, fluttering the coupons, reading each one aloud. "A dollar off on cereal. You should eat cereal; it's a grain, and you have to eat fiber."

He heard another horn but couldn't tell if it was behind or beside him. He looked at her again and back to the road. A truck was coming toward them in the other lanes. An intersection. A light. He put on his left signal and stepped on the gas.

"Red light, Don," she said quickly.

He turned the wheel, sweeping the car far left, crossing the lanes. The truck was on them. He didn't hear its horn or brakes. A car behind him blared its horn. She was holding up a coupon, looking at him, then looked to her right and saw the grill of the truck coming to her window.

"Don," she said.

Driving My Mother Crazy

September 16, 1992—it still felt like summer on that mid-September day in Baltimore. I was changing from my work clothes and into exercise clothes while I played back the messages on my answering machine. First: "Di, it's me." Larry's voice in his normal flat tones. Then the next message: "Hi, Di, it's Gloria. . . . Call me, okay? It's important." I could hear an odd, forced, upward inflection. Then one more message: "Hi, Diane, it's Sig, um, could you give me a call? I'm at Larry's. So . . . okay, give us a call as soon as you can."

I had phone calls from three siblings in one hour. I knew—or thought I knew—what was coming. Half-dressed, I kept looking at the phone and played the messages again. I wasn't calm, but I was trying to be.

I took several deep breaths. My mother must be dead. I took another breath and began to inventory myself. *What am I feeling? Am I okay?* I knew this day had to come. I hadn't worked out all the bumps with my mother, but we were good; we had come a long way in the past couple of years; therapy had helped. My mother was seventy-seven years old, and, I thought to myself, she had Donald. My mother had the gift of late-life romance. He was crazy, yes, but they were in love.

I dialed Larry's number. His answering machine picked up. I started to leave a message. "Hi, it's Diane. I got your message, what's—"

Then a voice. "Hi, Di, it's Sig." He was catching his breath. I was taking deep breaths again and bracing myself. I was waiting for him to tell me that our mother was dead.

"Diane, we have a problem," Sig began.

I thought, *A problem? That's a funny way to say it.*

"Di, Mum and Donald were in an accident. Mum was flown to shock trauma."

Whoa. Shift gears. An accident? Flown? I remember thinking, *This is gonna be harder than dead.*

"What do you mean?" I hoped my voice didn't sound as snippy to him as it did to me.

"Um," he began, and only some of the words made sense to me. "Mum and Donald . . . Route 4 . . . a big truck."

He must have said "big truck" several times before I said, "You mean a BIG truck?"

"Yeah, an eighteen-wheeler . . . passenger side . . . Mum . . . all broken . . . emergency crew . . . spleen, kidney, ribs . . . in a helicopter."

"A helicopter? Wow." That stopped me. "They brought a helicopter?"

"Yeah, it landed right on Route 4—they had to stop traffic for an hour."

He kept talking while I tried to adjust from "dead mother" to the immediately more complicated scenario.

I didn't want to ask if she was going to die. So I said, "Do they have to operate on her?"

"Diane, she's in shock trauma; that is surgery," Sig said. "They're keeping her there."

Oh, shit.

He kept talking. "Larry is there; Gloria is waiting for Tom to get home. . . . We don't know. . . . You should come say good-bye."

Here was my answer. I was being asked to come say good-bye to my mother.

"Okay, um . . . I have to call work." I couldn't figure out the fly or drive thing; my head couldn't seem to calculate the time or miles to Pittsburgh.

Finally, I had another thought and asked, "Is Donald dead?"

"No," Sig said, and then he sighed. "He's okay. He's fine. There's not a scratch on him, but they had to take him in, too. Di, he ran the light; he turned the car in front of the truck."

"So they arrested him?"

"No, but they had to take him to a hospital. He attacked the emergency medical crew. He thought they were trying to take Florence away from him."

Married Love

Donald loved my mother. With Florence, Donald had love, comfort, and acceptance. And he had family. He had all of that for ten years, and then one day he is driving down the road and turns his car into the path of a truck, and Florence is broken to pieces. He has—again—killed a woman he loves.

Imagine what it would feel like if you caused a car accident in which someone you loved dies. What would it be like to be right there? Can you feel that? And if you can feel that, then go to the next place: All you have ever wanted for the last forty years is to believe you are a decent person and have other people believe you are decent. You have lived all these years knowing you did an awful thing, and then there was brutality and torture. And finally, finally—you thought you were okay; someone loved you.

And now you are sitting on the side of the road because you caused an accident, and the woman you love—who loved you—may be dead. Another wife is dead.

The story almost ends there. Donald Watkins was taken from the scene of the accident in restraints. At the hospital he was sedated, and while he had no physical injuries, he was mute and disoriented. He was transferred to a nursing home in Brackenridge, Pennsylvania, where his diagnosis was "trauma-induced dementia." He died there four years later. His death certificate says "Parkinson's disease."

My mother, Florence Oklota Watkins, received emergency surgery in the shock trauma unit at Allegheny General Hospital in Pittsburgh, was maintained in the intensive care unit for many weeks, and then was moved to a nursing home in suburban Pittsburgh. She was a resident of the nursing home for almost ten years but never regained consciousness. Her death was described as cardiac failure following a traumatic brain injury.

CHAPTER FOURTEEN

There Are So Many Donalds

It is November 12, 2012. I am sitting on my couch having my morning coffee and reading *The New York Times*. A story on the front page catches my eye. Nicholas Kristof has written about a soldier, home from war: "A good man," according to neighbors, has "out of the blue" murdered his wife.

I skim the story—a vet has killed his wife. I go back and read it again. *This is Donald,* I think. *It's still Donald; all these years, and it's still Donald.*

This story is so familiar; a good man with a good family and good prospects has murdered his wife. His friends, neighbors, and employers say, "He was a good man." I put away the Donald story so long ago, but I remember these are the words in the front-page story of the *Washington Observer* in 1953.

But something has changed. This man Kristof is writing about is a veteran—like Donald—but the reporter is immediately asking if this vet experienced trauma or a head injury. He is asking if this is a straightforward murder or the result of trauma.

I had given up on the book about Donald, but now I can't. Maybe the story about Donald is about something more.

I shake my head and think, *It takes so long for people to understand this.* My search for Donald has to continue. I need to go to the experts again so I can connect what happened "then" to what is happening "now." As I talk to friends in the mental health profession and the yoga community, one expert's name comes up over and over.

Bessel van der Kolk

In late 2012, I attended the conference "Veterans, Trauma and Treatment" at Omega Institute in Rhinebeck, New York. The conference agenda focused on new approaches to healing trauma. There were keynote addresses and workshops with the luminaries of the trauma field including Bessel van der Kolk, Peter Levine, Roland McCraty, and Jon Kabat-Zinn.

I knew Donald's story was not unique. I wanted to know more about how military trauma works—what exactly happens? What can be done? And, with Thomas Szasz in the back of my mind, I thought, *Is trauma an illness?*

It didn't take long to surrender my researcher role. At Omega I came face-to-face with the realization that to make sense of Donald, I would have to take another step toward making sense of myself.

★ ★ ★

Bessel van der Kolk is the director of the Trauma Center in Boston, and he works with people who have experienced severe sexual trauma and trauma resulting from accidents. His clinical work includes veterans. I had met him a few years earlier at Kripalu, and at that time he had guided me to the research on body handlers, which helped me to understand how the daily life of the China Marines had left them traumatized.

So, here at Omega, I settle down in the classroom and begin to take notes. But a few minutes into his lecture, as van der Kolk starts talking about what happens to the body and brain, my breathing starts to slow down. He reveals that certainty of death is the key cause of trauma. I put my pen down and listen.

Van der Kolk shows a video clip of himself working with a woman who survived a horrific car accident, and as he describes the situation, he says the trauma she experienced was not a result of what happened to her car or the severe injuries to her body, but rather the crucial factor in the severity of her trauma was her certainty that she was going to die. *Click!* The feeling inside me is almost audible.

I had told the story of my day in Ambridge so many times, that nightmare day when Donald took control of the car, and I now remember my own words: "I knew I was going to die." But listening to van der Kolk, I understand what happened in a new way.

He explains that this belief is the criterion for trauma. "The traumatized person believes that death is imminent. He or she experiences mortal fear. That is what happens to victims of violent rape, victims of severe torture, and it is what happens in war."

Dr. van der Kolk describes trauma as pieces of residue that get stuck in the body and brain. "There is no narrative," he says, "only these pieces. The very nature of trauma is that the part of the brain that normally makes sense of experiences has been hijacked. You can't talk about trauma because the part of the brain that makes language and creates narrative shuts off. Our very vocabulary knows this. Every culture has a word for speechless or struck dumb.

"The trauma is not in the incident," he reminds us, "it is in the victim's nervous system. Only *after* the treatment and *after* healing can a narrative be created. This is why," van der Kolk says emphatically to a now very uncomfortable audience of clinicians, "asking a trauma victim to retell his or her story—what we call 'debriefing'—amounts to abuse and malpractice."

In trauma the rational mind has no access to the emotional brain. The connection is severed. One is simply furious or frightened for no reason. It is not—as we have imagined—that the cause is suppressed. One simply experiences sensation and reaction. The behaviors triggered by these out-of-order elements can make a person look and feel crazy, and they can behave very dangerously.

Now, again, I can hear Cliff Wells asking me, "Diane, do you know what hand-to-hand combat is?" And I recall the horror I felt as he explained the blades of the bayonets and the stabbing. But in my next thought, I am twelve years old, and my mother is coming at me with a knife. I am so scared but I am also completely focused. I know not to raise my hands; it would be bloody. I will myself into stillness while my mother hacks at my hair.

"You cannot reach the traumatized brain using reason," van der Kolk is saying, "but that is what most traditional therapies attempt to do with veterans. They try to reason with them, saying things like 'You don't have to be scared anymore' and 'There is nothing bad here; the war is over.' These approaches only make people feel crazier, because, of course, they know they're not at war, but their body, which is in charge, does not know that."

I walk across the Omega campus with van der Kolk after his lecture. "Does this happen in all wars?" I ask him.

"Yes," he says, and then he asks, "Do you know about George Washington's advice to his troops?"

"No, I don't."

"As the Revolutionary War came to an end, Washington recognized how damaged his men were by that war's trauma," van der Kolk explains. "Washington told them they were too damaged for city life. He told them to accept the land grants that were the 'disability pension' of that time and encouraged them to move to far rural places in this new country—what is now New Hampshire and Vermont—where they could make lives away from cities and crowded places. They needed to be away from people."

Trauma Sealed in Amber

Time passes. I keep writing. I talk to my therapist about Donald, my mother, and what I learned from van der Kolk. I still want to understand how trauma works and why it was true for those— like Donald and some of the China Marines—who did not see combat.

At the end of a cold winter day, I drive to the office of Loretta Malta, PhD. Her office is small, with a small couch and an overstuffed visitor's chair. She welcomes me in, and I sense her combination of personal warmth and cool boundary. I've worked with many therapists and I appreciate this combination.

As I sit down, I'm guessing that Malta is in her mid-forties. She has long brown hair, wears no makeup, and is dressed in simple clothes, a gray T-shirt and a black cardigan. Her eyes stop me. She has large, gray-blue eyes and she holds my gaze an extra second too long. Again that combination of warmth and assertion.

We sit down and she asks, "So you're writing a book about your stepfather and you have questions about military mental illness?" And the session begins.

Malta has the demeanor of a good teacher; she pulls a few papers from a file cabinet, and I can see the rows of slim files, each neatly labeled. She hands me a paper and says, "This is a list of the symptoms of PTSD," and she points to each one as she explains them.

I begin to tell her about Donald: the young Marine, the day he went "off his rocker" in Tientsin, and his admission to St. Elizabeths. I ask Malta what treatments Donald was likely to have received there in the late 1930s.

"He was probably treated as if he had schizophrenia," she explains.

I tell her that his diagnosis from China was dementia praecox—an early term for schizophrenia.

"Yes," she nods, "that was very common. Most of those vets and most World War II traumatized vets with PTSD were diagnosed with dementia praecox. At St. Elizabeths he could have had shock treatment, electroconvulsive therapy, but would also have had some talk therapy. Freud's ideas were common at that time, but mostly it was milieu therapy, which meant rest in a nice environment, the idea being that a soothing milieu was restful to the nerves and healing."

I tell her that I've seen some of the big state hospitals with their beautiful grounds—"Sheppard Pratt Hospital near my neighborhood in Baltimore was that style, a beautiful campus, farm and grounds, trees."

"Yes," Malta says, "time spent in nature was part of milieu therapy."

I tell her that most people talk about PTSD being a result of combat and that it comes from feeling imminent danger. "But," I explain, "that was not the case with the China Marines. For the most part they knew the Japanese wouldn't touch them, at least not in the early days before war was officially declared. They were witnesses; they stood guard. So why," I ask her, "was their trauma so bad if they didn't experience personal threat?"

Malta is shaking her head before I finish speaking. "But that's worse," she says, "that's much worse, and most of the guys I talk to will say that. They have much more regret, shame, and trauma because of situations where they couldn't act, didn't act. And think about it," she goes on, "these were Marines; the Marine culture is about not retreating, not leaving your dead, never leaving anyone. Marines are taught to protect, and then these men had to stand there and watch civilians being hurt and not intervene?"

She begins to describe the body's neurological responses to threat: fight, flight, or freeze. I can hear the good teacher in her.

"The flight response is trained out of Marines; freeze or fight is all that's left. But even if you go numb, your own numbness will torture you. You ask yourself, 'Who am I who can look at dead children or women and not feel anything? I'm a monster.'" She says, "Witnessing atrocities is much worse than being tortured."

Malta references the shooting at the elementary school in Newtown, Connecticut. "Look at how upsetting it was when we knew that twenty children had been killed, and your guys, these Marines like your stepfather, they were watching children being murdered for months. And how many do you think they saw, maybe twenty in a day? What happens if you do that?"

"And their duty," I tell her. "Every day they had to pick up body parts."

She nods; she knows about this. "And put them in piles?" she asks.

I nod.

"We forget what people see in these situations. We forget— or the public doesn't realize—what soldiers see and what first responders see. Think about the World Trade Center site . . . there was so much trauma for the workers because as they cleared rubble, they were finding parts of bodies. They don't talk about that."

"They are not like bodies in a funeral parlor," I respond.

She nods. "We have these situations that most people don't think about. In combat zones there are those who go in and fight, and many of them also have to sort through all the stuff after the battle. And others who are there to help. Even those who are not firing weapons may be seeing bodies all day long. And think about what they have to hear.

"Think about D-Day," Malta continues. "People think about courage and bravery, and they picture the soldiers running off the ship, but that wasn't the worst of it. Civilians don't know that those soldiers had to listen all night to the screams of their comrades. They could not come out to help them or they would have been shot. It was a beach in June covered with dying men who were torn apart, and they were screaming and begging for help. What happens to you if you listen to that for days?

"So," she says, picking up the list of PTSD symptoms again, "you have these intense feelings; it's very stressful. PTSD is a form of stress. The worst stress is having to relive the traumatic events over and over."

I ask Malta then, "But not all of those Marines came back like Donald; the men who I met and interviewed all had their issues for sure, but they didn't come home and kill. They had jobs and they had families and lives. What is different about them?"

Malta points to her checklist of symptoms again and says, "Most people who are traumatized will have these reactions to some extent. They will have bad memories and some flashbacks, and they will have some of the agitation and not be able to sleep. These symptoms happen to many people who are traumatized, but these might fade out over time. It takes time, but if they talk about it a little bit and if they mostly go on with life, the symptoms will mitigate.

"It's these," she says, pointing to the list again, "the numbing, isolating, distancing, and using alcohol or drugs—these cause the trouble. So maybe some of those other Marines who were in China with your stepfather, maybe they talked to people, maybe they stayed close to friends, maybe they kept busy or worked a lot, and that helped them."

What makes the biggest difference according to Malta is that they probably didn't drink to excess. "If you drink too much," she says as she points to the symptoms in the middle of the checklist again, "it is like sealing the trauma memories in amber."

"It's counterintuitive," I say. "We offer people a drink when they are under stress."

"Yes," she laughs. "We say, 'Have a brandy'—and that may be effective in the short term. It's instant relief, alcohol. It works fast. And think about what we have now, Xanax and Valium, the benzodiazepines. They affect the same brain areas as alcohol; you think it will help, but it's preserving it. Sadly, once again, that seals the trauma memories in amber.

"These Marines, like your stepfather, were rigorously trained to help and protect, but they could not. So what happens? You get angry, but where does that anger go? They hate themselves. Who doesn't save a child's life? Who doesn't save a pregnant woman? And so they go out at night."

"They are in Shanghai," I say, "Paris of the Orient."

"And . . ." she says, but I finish her sentence.

"They drink."

The result is lasting trauma that impacted so many lives for so long. And the cost of all this? I hesitate to say it, to put dollars to the numbers, but Malta says, "I like to say that war is only half the battle. We are still treating vets from World War II, and the war ended over fifty years ago. I see men from Korea. And these guys, like your stepfather, some of them still need help. It adds up."

She asks more about my mother and Donald. What did I notice about him? Did I see symptoms? I tell her about his rigidity and being "on the clock" and his insistence on watching his television show at a specific hour.

She smiles and says, "It's a leftover from good training. Think about it. We talk about precision, military precision. Marines and service personnel are trained to a really high standard—to maybe an 85 or 90 percent precision level, with the hope that in combat enough of that training will kick in. You don't need that kind of precision in civilian life. But Marines and other military personnel are trained to understand that precision means safety; they are told that over and over. Those drills are not for discipline; they are not just to assert authority. It's about safety.

"It becomes a kind of obsessive-compulsive disorder," she continues. "In the military that's a good thing; in civilian life it's a problem. Have your back to the wall, stay out of crowds, everything in its place, a television show at a certain time; yes, it sounds like Donald may have had some symptoms of PTSD."

I tell her that Donald lived alone in a cabin outside Pittsburgh after Farview. She is not surprised. Again she points to the symptoms on the PTSD chart: isolation, shutting down, and numbing.

"Your mother must have been an incredible woman for accepting him, with his story and who he was," Malta says. "He met her at the right time, though, I think," she goes on. "He was aging; he wouldn't have been able to keep up that isolated life much longer. The highest risk of suicide is in men over age sixty-five," she tells me.

"That's so sad," I say. "That's everyone's grandpa."

"Your mother provided a kind of milieu therapy for Donald. She accepted him as he was; she accepted his past; she helped him."

I can see from the windows that it's dark outside. It's time to go.

"These are really fine people, fine men." Malta gestures as if Donald is in the room with us. "Many people don't know that people in the military have longevity and loyalty. Compared to the general population, military personnel have marriages that last. They are well educated. They are really fine people."

I see color come into her face as she says this. I know this is why she is so good at her work.

"Most people don't know what fine people these are," she says again, "especially the Marines; they are so loyal and so caring." There are tears in her eyes.

★ ★ ★

CHAPTER FIFTEEN

Still Crazy After All These Years

In March of 2000, I receive an invitation to Thomas Szasz's eightieth birthday party, as promised. It won't be an ice-cream-and-cake affair, though. His party will be a symposium at SUNY Health Science Center, Syracuse. The title is "Liberty and/or Psychiatry?: 40 Years After the Myth of Mental Illness." The cochairs, Jeffrey Schaler, PhD, and Nelson Borelli, MD, have been advocates of Szasz's for many years. And so to prepare, I reread, again, *The Myth of Mental Illness.*

I arrive early and find a place to park, then I walk through the campus neighborhood to buy a coffee in a student café. As I drink my coffee, I think about all the places this quest for Donald has taken me. I smile to think of the Marines, the tour of St. Elizabeths, and now here for Thomas Szasz's birthday party. I bundle up again and walk to the university auditorium in the windy cold.

The cover of the printed program provides a quote from Szasz: "Respect for the individual and his choices forms the backbone of my moral and political position." I am slowly coming to understand what Szasz is about. I'm curious to see today's crowd and who these other Szasz supporters will be.

In the auditorium, people arrive and take their seats. I choose a spot halfway back to one side. I want to see the speakers, but I also want to watch Szasz; he is sitting in the front row. I anchor my spot with my coat and notebook and then walk down the steps to greet Dr. Szasz.

"Yes, yes, I remember you, Mrs. Cameron." He shakes my hand. "She's writing a book," he says to some men nearby. I smile and demur; I don't want to talk about Donald today.

Jeffrey Schaler calls the session to order and, for the next six hours, I listen and scribble notes as I learn so much about Thomas Szasz the psychiatrist, linguist, teacher, doctor, colleague, and friend.

The first speakers set the tone for the day. Three are from the Department of Psychiatry at SUNY Health Science Center, Syracuse. This is the department that tried to get Szasz kicked out of the profession and have his tenured professorship yanked after *The Myth of Mental Illness* was published. Their remarks include: "Thomas Szasz is the world's best-known and most widely read living psychiatrist"; "Tom's description of the concept of transference and his writings on schizophrenia are still regarded as the top of our field and are required reading for psychiatric students around the world"; and "He is an intellectual treasure, indispensable to the training of psychiatrists around the world."

I put down my pen. I hadn't even thought of this. He's more than the man who got Donald out of Farview, more than a challenging peer, and more than a thorn in the side of lawyers and shrinks; he's an expert psychiatrist and analyst.

Throughout the day, speakers parade to the podium. Some address Szasz directly, looking at him sitting in the front row.

Others, more formal, read from their prepared notes, transcripts that will later, most likely, be published and added to what surely must be lengthy curriculum vitae.

George Alexander, a law professor from California, speaks about involuntary commitment, or "the state's way of removing undesirables from the public." He explains that now, even though commitments are shorter in duration, they are more repetitive, making it easier to imprison people without due process. He talks about how we often use illness as a criterion to deprive people of their civil rights.

Jeffrey Schaler, one of the organizers and a psychologist and law professor, and also an advocate for decriminalization of drugs, speaks next. He reminds the audience that Thomas Szasz had predicted that the "therapeutic state" was and would be a great threat to liberty. He suggests that perhaps Americans like dependence and being told what to do.

Ron Leifer speaks next. He is a psychiatrist in private practice, trained under Szasz. He also speaks about involuntary commitment and how frequently it is still used. His point is that involuntary commitment could become a kind of social control, and he makes the comparison of how a psychiatrist declaring mental illness is like the church's declaration of demonic possession. He speaks of psychiatric survivors and indicates members of the audience who have traveled long distances to be here today to thank Szasz.

John Friedberg speaks before lunch. He is a neurologist from Berkeley, and he's an expert on electroshock treatment and a member of the Board of the American Academy of Electrodiagnostic Medicine. He refers to electroconvulsive therapy as "fraud, force, and fear" and describes the misuse of shock "treatments." He's seen a lot, stating that people between the ages of thirty months and eighty-eight years are still being shocked. "But," he says dryly, "what's a little brain damage, a seizure disorder, or permanent memory loss in the face of controlling behaviors that other people don't like?"

He makes the point also that electroconvulsive therapy is abuse. "Willful physical assault without consent is assault and battery," he says. He reminds the audience that there really is no such thing as inpatient consent because all it takes is two signatures to send someone to "permanent imprisonment."

The buffet lunch is in the next room, and I take a place at an end table and sit with two women from Massachusetts. One teaches literature to medical students in Boston. The other is a movement therapist. I tell her about the movement therapy I did with a therapist in Baltimore and how helpful it was. We talk about the various theories and how the field has developed over twenty years. They've read Szasz's books and have heard him talk many times. He's right about most of it, they say. I finish my lunch and walk outside again. I buy a newspaper and get some change for my parking meter. I'm glad for the cold air and a chance to move my legs.

Erwin Savodnik begins the seminar for the afternoon. He's a psychologist and professor of philosophy at UCLA. He's a perfect speaker to lift the crowd's energy after the lunch break. "A delusion is a false belief," he says. He talks about schizophrenia as the sacred cow of psychiatry. "Evidence of the illness is bad behavior."

The last speaker of the day is Peter Swales, a Freud historian, who calls himself a social archeologist. He talks about the epidemic of multiple personality disorder that followed the best-selling book *Sybil*—the woman who supposedly fragmented into sixteen "alters." Swales's research and follow-up on that case led to finding Shirley Mason, or "Sybil," alive and married in West Virginia and discovering that medication mismanagement and sexual abuse were part of her "therapy."

I walk back to my car and drive to the hotel. I have time for a shower and a quick read-through of today's notes. The big dinner is here at this hotel tonight.

In the ballroom of this old upstate hotel, the crystal chandelier glows, the candles in each flowered centerpiece flicker, and the murmured conversation and soft laughter are warm and congenial. This crowd is as pleased with itself as with its guest of honor. It is the end of a day of recognition, celebration, and gracious amends.

There are one or two men wearing tuxedos, but most of the men are in blazers or suits, and the women wear pants with colorful tunics or shawls, but some wear long, flowing dresses decorated with braided or pseudo-Native American designs.

Today's seminar honoring Szasz has been about the man and his work. Tonight for his party, this group of more than 100 people who gathered all day in the lecture hall seems transformed.

Over and over during the day, speakers took the podium to say, "Tom, we knew you were right" and "Now we understand." Several, among them notable psychiatrists, offered generously, "You've made us better at what we do." Time, commitment, and eighty years of a man's life are factored into their remarks.

During the cocktail hour we reintroduce ourselves and chat. It's an easy group to mingle with. "Are you a professor?" is the easiest opening line, or "Where are you from?" Today's group is, for the most part, from universities and medical centers on the East Coast, but some are here from the West Coast, and others have come from France and Germany. They are all here to toast this man who is credited with infuriating those who treat mental illness and being a champion for those who are mentally ill.

While his theories made the case that mental illness is a linguistic construct, Thomas Szasz worked endlessly to help people who were "incarcerated" in mental hospitals. He fought for their civil rights and due process.

"How do you know Tom Szasz?" a woman asks me as I join a small group at the vegetable and cheese table. "Are you a student?"

"No," I explain, munching carrots. "I'm writing a book about one of Dr. Szasz's former clients. It's about a man Dr. Szasz liberated from a state hospital," I reassure her, carefully choosing the word *liberated;* after all, this is libertarian headquarters tonight. Her smile returns. Szasz's followers and supporters also suffered the fallout of his controversial position. Years of defending Thomas Szasz's work had cost them, too.

This weekend is not only his celebration; it is their redemption. Some people in this room stood by him for forty years; several lost their academic positions and publishing opportunities because of their belief in his work. This gathering also means that these doctors, teachers, and scholars weren't crazy for saying to colleagues and students, "You must read Thomas Szasz."

At the end of dinner Jeffrey Schaler takes the podium to offer thanks, and he wishes Szasz a happy birthday. Later, when a large cake with many sparkling candles is wheeled into the ballroom, Szasz finally takes the microphone. People shush each other. This is the man they've come to see, the man they argued with, read about, apologized for, and championed for years.

He is tiny behind the podium. He starts to speak and then clears his throat to begin again, adjusting his voice for the large room.

"In 1798," he says, "Americans were confronted with the task of abolishing slavery peacefully and without violating the rights of others. They refused to face that daunting task, and we are still paying the price of their refusal. Now we face the task of abolishing psychiatric slavery. As Americans before us eventually replaced involuntary servitude—chattel slavery—with contractual relations between employers and employees, we seek to replace involuntary psychiatric slavery with contractual relations between caregivers and clients. Mental illness is a metaphor and an ideological justification for social control."

This, I realize, watching from the corner of the room, is Thomas Szasz's version of making a birthday wish.

Frenchy Continues to Write—2000

Frenchy's letters arrive every two weeks. In one he answers what I have asked over and over: why didn't he suffer battle fatigue or shell shock, especially after what he endured at the Palawan prison camp?

"I was so happy to be rescued," he writes, "so this was never a problem. Maybe it was my upbringing. Our conflicts weren't the glorious battles." He goes on, "There weren't any cameras where we were, and the history books never mention our piece of World War II."

I think it is true that temperament and upbringing—the factors that psychologists tell us are part of resilience—were key factors in Frenchy's emotional survival. He was battered in China and the Philippines, starved, beaten, and blinded before he was twenty-five years old, yet at eighty-seven he is still an outgoing optimist, always kind, and the perfect barkeep in the hospitality suite.

There was one moment, though, Frenchy told me, one time when he had a taste of what the other China Marines live with. Here is what Frenchy wrote:

> About three months after I came home, I had one flashback. It was a dream that several Jap guards had come to my home. I saw them coming up the front walk. As I ran down the hall to go out the

back door, I saw one of them standing with his back to the porch wall by the door, and as I ran by, I heard his rifle fire and I was hit in the back with the bullet. My feet flew out from under me, and I fell between two rows of roses in our backyard.

One taste and never another. You are the first one, except my wife, to hear of this incident. Some of the fellows do have problems, though. A few still attend weekly group therapy at the VA hospital.

That is, he means, his fellow Marines still attend therapy fifty-seven years later.

Redemption Song

It may seem obvious to you, but it was only after a decade of research, traveling to reunions, searching archives, filing multiple Freedom of Information Act requests, and finding the China Marines that one day it dawned on me that the reason I was working so hard to find Donald was that I needed to know how people survived terrible things. And each day of my pilgrimage, I was learning.

Donald Watkins killed two people, and he was abused, tortured, and shamed for years. The China Marines experienced trauma and moral injury; they witnessed civilian atrocities, saw their fellows brutally murdered, and yes, as Marines, they killed, too. Their struggles and injuries affected them for years. Two middle-aged attorneys didn't know for decades that the work they did as students had saved lives. Thomas Szasz was ridiculed for decades because he declared that people with mental illness deserved civil rights. Donald and Frenchy, Thomas Szasz, Josh and Roy, and Cliff and Bones—all of these people helped me to understand resilience and redemption.

CHAPTER SIXTEEN

Iambic Pentameter and the Meter of War

It's mid-January, and Vermont is sunny and snow-covered. I have taken a break from Donald and the Marines to visit Bennington College to hear the poet Robert Bly speak to the graduate writing students. It's bright and cold as I walk the short path to the lecture hall.

Bly has just begun to speak when I slip into the back of the darkened hall. I peel off my parka while my eyes adjust. He is talking about how structure is part of the message in any writing. He focuses on the early 1940s, his younger days, when he learned the formal shapes of poems and the rules of poetry. Strictness of form and careful structure were critical to the work they were all doing then.

"Prescribed forms were important because we were, at that time, writing about social madness. It was World War II," he says, and I lean forward in my seat. "We were writing about the war, bombing. America was at war on two sides of the world—it was a crazy time filled with chaos." Volatile content required strict form to contain it.

Bly reads to the college audience from Robert Frost. He tells us to listen to the form, explaining that we can hear the despair and emotional chaos in Frost's life in his poems. Then Bly waves the small book of Frost poems and says, "Frost chose to convey his life's words in iambic pentameter because it just barely contains the chaos."

I lean back in my seat and put my feet up on the rail in front of me. As I listen to Bly describe the war and chaos of that time, I think of Donald, Frenchy, and my other China Marines. They had lived in chaos; they were part of the social madness. They were young, away from home for the first time. They had been at sea for weeks on the USS *Chaumont*. When they finally neared their exotic destination, ready for the promised worldly adventures, the ship pulled into a harbor full of floating human bodies. Their first job on Chinese soil was to go out each day, after the Japanese bombs had struck and the Japanese soldiers had tortured civilians, and pick up the dead bodies.

I think about that so often. For most of us, our picture of a dead body comes from a relative we've seen in a funeral home, or maybe a visit to a deathbed in a hospital. But those young Marines faced the dead in parts and pieces—heads, arms, and torsos separated and tossed about. Their job was to pick up the body parts and load them on trucks. Every day. How could they not go mad?

Robert Bly asks this audience of aspiring writers if they can let go of form or "at least the overused iambic pentameter." He explains that we learned this rhythmic pattern from the Greeks, who used it to express irony.

This is news. What do we miss in literature when we don't know that? What do we miss when we don't know our military history? What do we miss if we don't know those young Marines were not allowed to engage the Japanese, that all they could do was watch people get torn apart, and then pick up the pieces?

A woman sitting across the room is waving her hand. Before Bly can call on her, she blurts out, "But form can either be a cage that is outside of us and therefore limiting us, or we can see it as a support, as something internal like a skeleton that provides structure, that allows us to hang things on it."

I think of Frenchy. What structure allowed him to survive in China and the Palawan prison? How did he structure his experience so that he could come home more or less intact? Was it simply youth? Religion? Marine esprit de corps?

I think about Cliff Wells, and I remember him telling me about being a young man with no job. "It was the Depression, Diane, no one could get a job." So he and two friends went off to join the Marines. He was nervous. Would they get in? He was selected. He would go to China: foreign, exotic, and yes, the girls. I have learned about the mama-san houses in China, which provided rice and meat and, well, a little "piece." Of course Cliff doesn't use that kind of language. He says, "The Marines made sure we had everything; providing all the things a young soldier needs to keep him happy, girls of course, providing pleasure."

What part did pleasure and sex play in counterbalancing the chaos? In facing down the madness? Picking up shredded body parts by day, then going to the mama-san house for sex and dinner at night?

I wonder now how aware those young men were of the greater geopolitical picture. There was war coming to the Pacific, and it would get much worse for all of them. Picking up body parts was a prelude, preparation for what was to come. Very soon they would do their own killing.

On the telephone Cliff told me about the medals he had received for hand-to-hand combat. Hand-to-hand sounds so innocuous. Like shaking hands or arm-wrestling. I keep hearing Cliff say, "Well, Diane, you look at a man who is going to kill you, and you kill him first. You stab him over and over with your bayonet."

How could we expect our soldiers to survive that?

Not everyone makes it out. Donald was broken and crazy, but he was also strong and persistent. It was both his temperament and his Marine training that allowed him to survive the trauma he experienced and the trauma he inflicted.

Perhaps that's the key: how well a person can contain the chaos of their life, the chaos of heartbreak or war or murder or mental illness. If there is a form—linguistic, emotional, or spiritual—they survive. Maybe some Marines, like Frenchy, possess a form, an iambic pentameter, that courses through their lives, keeping their chaos in check. But for others, like Donald, their meter is more fragile, more unmanageable, and the chaos spills over in unruly and violent waves. These waves crash into other lives—Donald's wife's, her mother's, then my mother's, and then into mine.

Maybe this is Donald's gift to me—an unexpected one from a man whose measure I am still taking—to look at the meter of my own life, valuing those things that keep me from chaos and, as much as I can, counting on the good.

Bill Nash—Stress, Combat, Psychiatry, and the Marines

In May of 2015, I read the book *God Is Not Here* by Lieutenant Colonel Bill Edmonds. It is a memoir and the story of his experience as the lone American embedded in an Iraqi/Kurdish military detention facility. Edmonds was there at the same time as—and because—United States soldiers were being sent to prison for what they did in Abu Ghraib.

His assignment was to supervise the "debriefing" of Iraqi prisoners to elicit confessions and information on other terrorists they might be working with. Edmonds describes the moral dilemma that grew in him as one of being present in the prison to prevent torture while slowly coming to understand that the terrorists in that prison would not give up information without "pressure," and that if the crucial information was not secured, many innocent people would die—and they would die terrible deaths.

The question and controversy in Edmonds's book is whether what he witnessed in 2005 was related to his severe breakdown in Germany six years later. In the introduction to *God Is Not Here*, Dr. William Nash suggests that Edmonds's story is not about PTSD but instead about moral injury and moral repair.

I know, as I read the introduction, Bill Nash is the guy I need to talk to. I have been hoping to find a military expert on military trauma to give me today's psychiatric perspective on Donald. I want to know if a current military psychiatrist would agree with me that Donald's behavior, and the murders, resulted from PTSD.

But I worry whether someone like Nash would give me the time of day. And would he wonder, as indeed I have, if I am crazy for spending all these years piecing together Donald's life? But I also realize, if anyone knows trauma and the Marines, it is this doctor. So I google him and he is listed as Bill Nash, MD, CAPT, MC, USN (Ret.), Former Director of Combat and Operational Stress Control Programs for the US Marine Corps and Assistant Clinical Professor of Psychiatry at the University of California, San Diego.

Yes, I am intimidated, but *this* is the guy.

So I start writing and emailing and get nothing back. I can't tell where he works—he has many projects in many locations. I find him on LinkedIn and leave a message. Nothing.

A month later I am on LinkedIn again, and there is a message from Bill Nash. He says he is happy to talk and leaves a phone number. Now I freeze. I'm picturing a lot of brass and bars on navy blue. I write back and set a time to talk, but I tell him I am happy to come to Washington to meet him in person. I suspect it will be easier for me to talk about Donald face-to-face and convince this guy that I am seriously committed to my China Marines.

The hour for the phone call arrives, and I am ill with nerves. I close my office door and sit at my desk; my arms are crossed, my legs are twisted under me, and I am bound by tension. *What if he is stern? What if he is rolling his eyes? What if he's just not nice?* But then he answers the phone, and I immediately know he is nice when he says, "Diane, you have a great story to tell."

One week later I wake at three o'clock in the morning to go to the Albany airport to take the five o'clock flight to the Baltimore-Washington airport. From there I take a bus, then a train, and then two subways, and then walk a few blocks to our meeting in Fairfax, Virginia. I'm early, so I walk around and around the block, finally going into The Willow restaurant to wait for Dr. Nash. I am still wishing I could get up and leave when I see a casually dressed, tall, bearlike man approach the hostess, and I know this is Bill Nash. I walk toward him, and we hug. It just feels right. His warmth and humor are right there; he has a warm smile, beautiful eyes, and full attention.

Bill asks me, "How long did you know Donald?" and we are off. Two hours later, after salads and chicken and a caramel cake that the waiter tells us was baked by an eleven-year-old pastry savant, our nonstop talking slows down. We have covered trauma, Marine training, suicide of veterans, and why wounded-warrior programs continue to keep veterans at a distance from the civilian population. Nash is eloquent about the ways the civilian population is in denial about what we ask soldiers to do for us when we send them to war. I ask him about the use of clinical debriefing and using rituals for healing, and he says we have to stay with the science.

Nash says that the truth is, for all the theories we have seen over the years about trauma and PTSD, "many of them are conflicting—we still don't know who will get PTSD and who will be okay." For years we assumed people who had been abused as children would be at higher risk, but that doesn't prove out. In fact, for some people, having dealt with abuse or trauma early in life becomes a protective factor in later trauma.

Nash has read the copy of Donald's medical records I had sent to him. He asks me if I ever felt Donald was dangerous, and I tell him about the day in the car in Ambridge.

"So it was that close to the surface, his anger. And your mother, was she happy?"

I tell him that she was, and they had ten years of a pretty good marriage, and he shakes his head.

"Is that old age or trauma or mental illness?" I ask him.

"Yes, there was damage in China, a head injury of some kind—but witnessing the Japanese atrocities, that was likely his real damage or the trigger for an underlying disorder."

We talk about St. Elizabeths. Nash knows the history. I ask about "shock treatment."

"Yes—that can be a very good treatment if done right. It's the seizure that produces the cure—the seizure, not the electrical current or the insulin injections—the seizure is what can be curative."

I can tell that Nash likes this subject, the history of military trauma; this is his area. I was right: This is the guy to talk to. I ask Nash about trauma in earlier wars—in World War I and the Civil War. Military trauma looked different then; it showed in the body—all that twitching and jerking, all those Parkinson's-like symptoms—the somatic responses.

I explain my theory—that we didn't have words, we had no language for war trauma, and so no one could talk about it.

"And so," says Nash, "the trauma showed in the body. While we understood it as a conversion disorder, that also led to the additional betrayal of veterans. Some military doctors tried to shame the vets out of the trauma. They misunderstood the concept of 'conversion disorder,' thinking it meant 'made up,' and they would use aversive treatments, cruel speech, getting right up in the vet's face and screaming and accusing him of faking until the veteran broke down or reacted. If the numbed or emotionally paralyzed vet reacted violently, then the doctor could declare him 'cured' because he got him to react. It was cruel."

Then he tells me something that is a surprise. "In the past we assumed trauma occurred because the soldier was afraid. But now our research is showing that the number-one emotion in battle is not fear. Rather, the key emotions at play in combat are love, honor, and shame."

I'd heard other Marines talk about love. The older veterans said that what kept them on the battlefield was not love of flag or country but rather love for their fellows. And honor makes sense, too—it's drummed into recruits from day one of boot camp and every day after that. But shame was a surprise, and it was a particular thing about shame. Not just shame in the way that shame might motivate you to not retreat from battle, but shame as fuel for violence, as a thing that motivates a man to kill—the need to be violent as a way to *extinguish* shame.

Something clicked for me when Bill Nash talked about shame as an emotion that can fuel killing. I remembered reading another expert on shame, James Gilligan, MD, who wrote about the shame-violence connection. In his book *Violence: Reflections on a National Epidemic,* Gilligan, an expert on prison psychiatry, wrote: "The emotion of shame is the primary or ultimate cause of all violence whether toward others or toward the self." In his book and in his work as an expert witness, Gilligan shows that we are missing the extreme vulnerability underlying the most horrendous violent acts. This occurs in civilian life and in military affairs.

CHAPTER SEVENTEEN

Never Leave Your Dead

Even now I can't tell you what anyone should have done differently. I'd like to think, as I so often fantasize, that if I came upon a man as broken as Donald, I'd get the hell out of the way. I have imagined that if, as an adult, I came across a family that was in the straits we were in back then, I'd know what to do. But the painful fact is that I don't know.

As I have lived through the writing of this story, I can still feel the very confines of the cage I am trying to write my way out of. I can point to the blood on the floor: Donald's, his wife's, my mother's, and mine, too.

The shocking thing about the day Donald took control of my car—I now realize—is not what Donald did but what my mother did not do. She never reacted. My mother, who had cut off my hair in a Dexedrine haze, who was both seductive and cruel to my brothers, who had been abused as a child and then went on to abuse her children, had simply looked the other way.

That is the other thing I have had to come to terms with: loving and being loved by a mother who was abused and abusive. A woman who likely never accepted herself but could love a man who had murdered his wife.

Over the years I've met people who did not survive the abuse in their lives. They were defeated by depression, addiction, or suicide. Or they succumbed to mental illness. But I know others—truly fierce people—who are recovering. And there is something else I know: there can be gifts from a painful childhood.

The skills I use in my work today came out of that horrible part of my life. I have a powerful intuition—the ability to anticipate what people need and feel. I have been told so many times that I am "calm in a crisis," but now, when I realize how I acquired that skill, it makes me sad. I've seen colleagues reduced to tears over problems like losing an important file or a late proposal. For me, being chased through the house at three o'clock in the morning by a woman in a manic rage, waving a knife, is a problem. Anything else is just a situation.

I'm proud of my survival. But like Donald, it's a mixed bag. Despite what the bumper sticker says, it *is* too late to have a happy childhood. So I take the whole package, grieve the losses, celebrate the gains, and work around the scar tissue.

Whenever I imagine Donald in the years before he met my mother, I think about what happened in 1953 in that kitchen in Western Pennsylvania. Today the world is so full of therapy, self-help, and social services that it's hard to imagine a time and place where a man could be so troubled and no one would see it or offer help.

Should Donald have been put away for his entire life? No. Am I glad Szasz liberated him? Yes. And am I glad that my mother saved him, too? Well, that moves the question from the theoretical to the personal. I am glad my mother found a man who could see her beauty. But with that she also got a difficult man.

Each time I am asked, "Were you afraid of Donald?" I hesitate. I think I should have a clear answer, but I don't.

I understand why people ask that question, though. Donald killed two women when he was younger. But I knew him when he was old. I have written a book about this man, but I still feel myself hesitate.

What is in that pause? Maybe it's grief. I do feel grief when I imagine Donald locked away all those years, especially now that I know what a horrific place Farview was. And Donald knew what he lost. He lived with the realization that he had killed the woman he loved. Many of us know what it is to lose someone to an accident or an illness, but imagine being the agent of your own loss. That could make you crazy.

We've come so far in our understanding of mental illness and trauma, but it also seems as if we haven't moved an inch. The stigma is pervasive. Trauma is an injury that accrues with every war. The language of trauma is changed by political and economic factors that affect how we speak about—and how we treat—those who experience trauma.

So what do I feel? Spin the wheel. I feel it all, but—and maybe this is the small difference that keeps me on this side of shock therapy and clozapine—I feel these things sequentially, not simultaneously. Donald felt love, hate, anger, fear, and powerful grandiosity all at once. Out of that amalgam, he concocted a murderous logic that let him both kill and survive nearly being killed.

Donald Watkins died in 1996, but the heart of his story is in today's news. Currently, 2.6 million soldiers are returning home from war—the greatest number since Vietnam. Today, somewhere in the United States a family is struggling. Today, a veteran is contemplating suicide or even homicide. The "Donalds" are still with us. And we still don't understand.

We want men and women like Donald Watkins to be crazy or sane, criminal or innocent, good or bad, but few people fit those categories. We want life to be black or white, but it is mostly gray. Donald Watkins is a spokesperson for the gray.

Ships That Pass in the Night

"Ships that pass in the night." I'd used that phrase from Longfellow's poem many times. I assumed it referenced things that don't communicate with each other. Then, one day I read the rest of the line: "Ships that pass in the night and speak each other in passing." I was struck by what seemed a common misunderstanding. When people say, "They were like ships that pass in the night," don't they mean there is no communication? But what if ships passing in the night do, in fact, communicate? What if they "speak each other in passing"? A ship at sea can signal across miles of dark water to a mighty and contained other. In nautical communication, those few lights that flash a ship's name, course, and condition could be a reassuring connection.

Maybe Donald and I are like that. I came to know him most fully after his death. When he was alive, we were at a remove. When I visited, we ate, watched television, and went shopping. But my mother was always between us, keeping up a patter to smooth over any discomfort.

Donald and I are like those ships, two contained entities, partially submerged. Across a dark sea we passed each other. Now, across death and time, I speak to him in passing.

ACKNOWLEDGMENTS AND THANKS

My journey to Donald took more than twenty years and so, of course, I have many people and organizations to thank. At the top of the list are the United States China Marines—all of them—in gratitude for their service, and specifically Joseph "Frenchy" Dupont, Cliff Wells, George Howe, Dante Caruso, Pat Hitchcock, Fred "Bones" Konieg, and Glenn McDole.

Thank you to libraries and librarians, specifically at the Carnegie Library of Pittsburgh; the Washington County, Pennsylvania, Public Library; the US Naval Archives; the United States Marine Corps Archives, Marine Corps History and Museums Division; the China Marine Association; the Guilderland, New York, Public Library; and the Crossett Library at Bennington College.

A big thank you to the staff at Central Recovery Press for believing this book will help others. Special thanks to Valerie Killeen, Patrick Hughes, and Janet Ottenweller for making me write better and laugh more. I'm honored to be part of the CRP team.

My gratitude to the teachers, friends, and therapists who coaxed this story out of me and helped me put it back together: Rob Kanigel, Sven Birkerts, Susan Cheever, Lucy Grealy, Annie Decker, Ed Sanders, Marion Roach Smith, Mike Breslin, Nancy Kowalczyk, Stephanie Gibson, Brigid Globensky, Phyllis Trout, and Johnell Bushel. And thank you to the organizations that gave me space and solitude to dive deep: Millay Colony for the Arts and Bennington College.

Thank you to the many experts who helped me to understand trauma, war, and redemption. Among them: Bessel van der Kolk, MD; William Nash, MD; Nisha Money, MD, MPH; Iris Chang; Myles Schwartz, PhD; Loretta Malta, PhD; and Peter Cameron, PhD.

And special recognition for the men who saved Donald's life—and the lives of many others: Thomas Szasz, Roy Diamond, and Josh Goldblum.

My deepest thanks to the family that surrounds me today: Susan Griffiths, Stephen Cope, Anne Pascone, Kathy Catlin, Diane Segal, Betsy Voss, and especially my husband, David Pascone—who believed in my recovery and my writing. You have shown me that love can heal.

THE SYMPTOMS OF POST-TRAUMATIC STRESS DISORDER

The list below summarizes the key symptoms of PTSD and the personality changes that mark its severe forms. All may be understood as the persistence of past traumatic experiences in the present physiology, psychology, and social relatedness of the survivor. The symptoms can range from mild to devastating, and not everyone will have all the symptoms at the same time.

- Impaired mental function—primarily in memory and trustworthy perception.

- Persistent mobilization of the body and of the mind for lethal danger, with the potential for explosive violence.

- Persistence and activation of combat survival skills in civilian life.

- Chronic health problems stemming from chronic mobilization of the body for danger.

- Persistent expectation of betrayal and exploitation; destruction of the capacity for social trust.

- Persistent preoccupation with both the enemy and the veteran's own military/governmental authorities.

- Alcohol and other drug abuse.

- Suicidal ideation, despair, isolation, and meaninglessness.

RESOURCES FOR VETERANS AND THEIR FAMILIES AND FRIENDS

If you are a veteran, or someone you care about is a veteran, and you would like information about help that is available, please contact one or more of the organizations listed below.

- **The National Center for PTSD**
  www.PTSD.va.gov

- **The Trauma Center, Boston, Massachusetts**
  617-232-1303

- **The Department of Veterans Affairs**
  800-827-1000 for a local contact

- **The Vet Center** (local programs of the VA)
  Call your local VA.

- **Alcoholics Anonymous**
  www.aa.org, or call directory assistance.

- **Al-Anon Family Groups**
  www.al-anon.org, or call directory assistance.

- **American Foundation for Suicide Prevention**
  888-333-AFSP

- **Samaritans USA** (suicide prevention)
  800-273-TALK

- **Sidran Institute**
  (survivors of trauma/family members)
  www.sidran.org

- **Soldier On**
  www.wesoldieron.org

- **Give Back Yoga Foundation** (programs
  for veterans)
  www.givebackyoga.org

- **The National Domestic Violence Hotline**
  800-799-7233 or 800-787-3224 (TTY)

- **The China Marine Website**
  www.chinamarine.org